The Countess of Albany

The Countess of Albany

Vernon Lee

MINT EDITIONS

The Countess of Albany was first published in 1884.

This edition published by Mint Editions 2021.

ISBN 9781513295671 | E-ISBN 9781513297170

Published by Mint Editions®

 MINT
EDITIONS

minteditionbooks.com

Publishing Director: Jennifer Newens
Design & Production: Rachel Lopez Metzger
Project Manager: Micaela Clark
Typesetting: Westchester Publishing Services

Contents

PREFACE

In preparing this volume on the Countess of Albany (which I consider as a kind of completion of my previous studies of eighteenth-century Italy), I have availed myself largely of Baron Alfred von Reumont's large work *Die Gräfin von Albany* (published in 1862); and of the monograph, itself partially founded on the foregoing, of M. St. René Taillandier, entitled *La Comtesse d'Albany*, published in Paris in 1862. Baron von Reumont's two volumes, written twenty years ago and when the generation which had come into personal contact with the Countess of Albany had not yet entirely died out; and M. St. René Taillandier's volume, which embodied the result of his researches into the archives of the Musée Fabre at Montpellier; might naturally be expected to have exhausted all the information obtainable about the subject of their and my studies. This has proved to be the case very much less than might have been anticipated. The publication, by Jacopo Bernardi and Carlo Milanesi, of a number of letters of Alfieri to Sienese friends, has afforded me an insight into Alfieri's character and his relations with the Countess of Albany such as was unattainable to Baron von Reumont and to M. St. René Taillandier. The examination, by myself and my friend Signor Mario Pratesi, of several hundreds of Ms. letters of the Countess of Albany existing in public and private archives at Siena and at Milan, has added an important amount of what I may call psychological detail, overlooked by Baron von Reumont and unguessed by M. St. René Taillandier. I have, therefore, I trust, been able to reconstruct the Countess of Albany's spiritual likeness during the period—that of her early connection with Alfieri—which my predecessors have been satisfied to despatch in comparatively few pages, counterbalancing the thinness of this portion of their biographies by a degree of detail concerning the Countess's latter years, and the friends with whom she then corresponded, which, however interesting, cannot be considered as vital to the real subject of their works.

Besides the volumes of Baron von Reumont and M. St. René Taillandier, I have depended mainly upon Alfieri's autobiography, edited by Professor Teza, and supplemented by Bernardi's and Milanesi's *Lettere di Vittorio Alfieri*, published by Le Monnier in 1862. Among English books that I have put under contribution, I may mention Klose's *Memoirs of Prince Charles Edward Stuart* (Colburn, 1845), Ewald's *Life and Times of Prince Charles Stuart* (Chapman and Hall, 1875), and Sir Horace Mann's *Letters to Walpole*, edited by Dr. Doran. A review, variously attributed to Lockhart and to Dennistoun, in the *Quarterly* for 1847, has been all the more useful to me as I have been unable to procure, writing in Italy, the *Tales of the Century*, of which that paper gives a masterly account.

For various details I must refer to Charles Dutens' *Mémoires d'un Voyageur qui se repose* (Paris, 1806); to Silvagni's *La Corte e la Società Romana nel secolo XVIII*; to Foscolo's *Correspondence*, Gino Capponi's *Ricordi* and those of d'Azeglio; to Giordani's works and Benassù Montanari's *Life of Ippolito Pindemonti*, besides the books quoted by Baron Reumont; and for what I may call the general pervading historical colouring (if indeed I have succeeded in giving any) of the background against which I have tried to sketch the Countess of Albany, Charles Edward and Alfieri, I can only refer generally to what is now a vague mass of detail accumulated by myself during the years of preparation for my *Studies of the Eighteenth Century in Italy*.

My debt to the kindness of persons who have put unpublished matter at my disposal, or helped me to collect various information, is a large one. In the first category, I wish to express my best thanks to the Director of the Public Library at Siena; to Cavaliere Guiseppe Porri, a great collector of autographs, in the same city; to the Countess Baldelli and Cavaliere Emilio Santarelli of Florence, who possess some most curious portraits and other relics of the Countess of Albany, Prince Charles Edward, and Alfieri; and also to my friend Count Pierre Boutourline, whose grandfather and great-aunt were among Madame d'Albany's friends. Among those who have kindly given me the benefit of their advice and assistance, I must mention foremost my friend Signor Mario Pratesi, the eminent novelist; and next to him the learned Director of the State Archives of Florence, Cavaliere Gaetano Milanese, and Doctor Guido Biagi, of the Biblioteca Vittorio Emanuel of Rome, without whose kindness my work would have been quite impossible.

Florence,
March 15, 1884

I

THE BRIDE

On the Wednesday or Thursday of Holy Week of the year 1772 the inhabitants of the squalid and dilapidated little mountain towns between Ancona and Loreto were thrown into great excitement by the passage of a travelling equipage, doubtless followed by two or three dependent chaises, of more than usual magnificence.

The people of those parts have little to do now-a-days, and must have had still less during the Pontificate of His Holiness Pope Clement XIV and we can imagine how all the windows of the unplastered houses, all the black and oozy doorways, must have been lined with heads of women and children; how the principal square of each town, where the horses were changed, must have been crowded with inquisitive townsfolk and peasants, whispering, as they hung about the carriages, that the great traveller was the young Queen of England going to meet her bridegroom; a thing to be remembered in such world-forgotten places as these, and which must have furnished the subject of conversation for months and years, till that Queen of England and her bridegroom had become part and parcel of the tales of the "Three Golden Oranges," of the "King of Portugal's Cowherd," of the "Wonderful Little Blue Bird," and such-like stories in the minds of the children of those Apennine cities. The Queen of England going to meet her bridegroom at the Holy House of Loreto. The notion, even to us, does savour strangely of the fairy tale.

What were, meanwhile, the thoughts of the beautiful little fairy princess, with laughing dark eyes and shining golden hair, and brilliant fair skin, more brilliant for the mysterious patches of rouge upon the cheeks, and vermilion upon the lips, whom the more audacious or fortunate of the townsfolk caught a glimpse of seated in her gorgeous travelling dress (for the eighteenth century was still in its stage of pre-revolutionary brocade and gold lace and powder and spangles) behind the curtains of the coach? Louise, Princess of Stolberg-Gedern, and ex-Canoness of Mons, was, if we may judge by the crayon portrait and the miniature done about that time, much more of a child than most women of nineteen. A clever and accomplished young lady, but, one would say, with, as yet, more intelligence and acquired pretty little habits and ideas than character; a childish woman of the world, a bright, light handful of thistle-bloom. And thus, besides the confusion, the unreality due to precipitation of events and change of scene, the sense that she had (how long ago—days, weeks, or years? in such a state time becomes a great muddle and mystery) been actually married by proxy, that she had come the whole way from Paris, through Venice and across the sea, besides being in this dream-like, phantasmagoric condition, which must have made all things seem light—it is probable that the young lady had scarcely sufficient consciousness of herself as a grown-up, independent, independently feeling and thinking creature, to feel or think very strongly over her situation. It was the regular thing for girls of Louise of Stolberg's rank to be put through a certain amount of rather vague convent education, as she had been at Mons; to be put through a certain amount of balls and parties; to be put through the formality of betrothal and marriage; all this was the half-conscious dream—then would come the great waking up. And Louise of Stolberg was, most likely, in a state of feeling like that which comes to us with the earliest light through the blinds: pleasant, or unpleasant? We know not which; still drowsing, dreaming, but yet strongly conscious that in a moment we shall be awake to reality.

There was, nevertheless, in the position of this girl something which, even in these circumstances, must have compelled her to think, or, at all events, to meditate, however confusedly, upon the present and the future. If she had in her the smallest spark of imagination she must have felt, to an acute degree, the sort of continuous surprise, recurring like the tick of a clock, which haunts us sometimes with the fact that it really does just happen to be ourselves to whom some curious lot, some rare combination of the numbers in life's lottery, has come. For the man whom she was going to marry—nay, to whom, in a sense, she was married already—the unknown whom she would see for the first time that evening, was not the mere typical bridegroom, the mere man of rank and fortune, to whom, whatever his particular individual shape and name, the daughter of a high-born but impoverished house had known herself, since her childhood, to be devoted.

Louise Maximilienne Caroline Emanuele, daughter of the late Prince Gustavus Adolphus of Stolberg-Gedern, Prince of the Empire, who had died, a Colonel of Maria Theresa, in the battle of Leuthen; and of Elisabeth Philippine, Countess of Horn, born at Mons in

Hainaut, the 20th September 1752, educated there in a convent, and subsequently admitted to the half-ecclesiastic, half-worldly dignity of Canoness of Ste. Wandru in that town: Louise, Princess of Stolberg, now in her twentieth year, had been betrothed, and, a few weeks ago, married by proxy in Paris to Charles Edward Stuart, known to history as the Younger Pretender, to popular imagination as Bonnie Prince Charlie, and to society in the second half of the eighteenth century as the Count of Albany. The match had been made up hurriedly—most probably without consulting, or dreaming of consulting, the girl—by her mother, the dowager Princess Stolberg, and the Duke of Fitz-James, Charles Edward's cousin. The French Minister, Duc d'Aiguillon, in one of those fits of preparing Charles Edward as a weapon against England, which had more than once cost the Pretender so much bitterness, and the Court of Versailles so much brazenly endured shame, had intimated to the Count of Albany that he had better take unto himself a wife. Charles Edward had more than once refused; this time he accepted, and his cousin Fitz-James looked around for a possible future Queen of England. Now it happened that the eldest son of Fitz-James, the Marquis of Jamaica and Duke of Berwick, had just married Caroline, the second daughter of the widow of Prince Gustavus Adolphus of Stolberg-Gedern; so that the choice naturally fell upon this lady's elder sister, Louise of Stolberg, the young Canoness of Ste. Wandru of Mons.

The alliance, short of royal birth, was, in the matter of dignity, all that could be wished; the Stolbergs were one of the most illustrious families of the Holy Roman Empire, in whose service they had discharged many high offices; the Horns, on the other hand, were among the most brilliant of the Flemish aristocracy, allied to the Gonzagas of Mantua, the Colonna, Orsinis, the Medina Celis, Croys, Lignes, Hohenzollerns, and the house of Lorraine, reigning or quasi-reigning families; and Louise of Stolberg's mother was, moreover, on the maternal side, the grand-daughter of the Earl of Elgin and Ailesbury, a Bruce, and a staunch follower of King James II. Such had been the inducements in the eyes of the Duke of Fitz-James; and therefore in the eyes of Charles Edward, for whom he was commissioned to select a wife. The inducements to the Princess of Stolberg had been even greater. Foremost among them was probably the mere desire of ridding herself, poor and living as she was on the charity of the Empress-Queen, of another of the four girls with whom she had been left a widow at twenty-five. It had been a great blessing to get the two eldest girls, Louise and Caroline, educated, housed for a time, and momentarily settled in the world by their admission to the rich and noble chapter of Ste. Wandru: it must have been a great blessing to see the second girl married to the son of Fitz-James; it would be a still greater one to get Louise safely off her hands, now that the third and fourth daughters required to be thought of. So far for the desirability of any marriage. This particular marriage with Prince Charles Edward was, moreover, such as to tempt the vanity and ambition of a lady like the widowed Princess of Stolberg, conscious of her high rank, and conscious, perhaps painfully conscious of the difficulty of living up to its requirements. The Count of Albany's grandfather had been King of England; his father, the Pretender James, had lived with royal state in his exile at Rome, recognised as reigning Sovereign by the Pope, and even, every now and then, by France and Spain. No Government had recognised Charles Edward as King of England; but, on the other hand, Charles Edward had virtually been King of Scotland during the '45; he had been promised the help of France to restore him to his rights; and although that help had never been satisfactorily given in the past, who could tell whether it might not be given at any moment in the future? The ups and downs of politics brought all sorts of unexpected necessities; and why should the French Government, which had ignominiously kidnapped and bundled off Charles Edward in 1748, have sent for him again only a year ago, have urged him to marry, unless it had some scheme for reinstating him in England? The Duke of Fitz-James had doubtless urged these considerations; he had not laid much weight on the fact that Charles Edward was thirty-two years older than his proposed wife; still less is it probable that he had bade the Princess of Stolberg consider that his royal kinsman was said to be neither of very good health, nor of very agreeable disposition, nor of very temperate habits; or, if such ideas were presented to the Princess Stolberg, she put them behind her. Be it as it may, these were matters for the judicious consideration of a mother; not, certainly, for the thoughts of a daughter. The judicious mother decided that such a match was a good one; perhaps, in her heart, she was even overwhelmed by the glory which this daughter of hers was permitted by Heaven to add to all the glories of the illustrious Stolbergs and Horns. Anyhow, she accepted eagerly; so eagerly as to forget both gratitude and prudence: for so far from consulting her benefactress, Maria Theresa, about the advisability of this marriage, or asking her sovereign permission for a step which might draw upon the Empress-Queen some disagreeable diplomatic correspondence with England, the Princess of Stolberg kept the matter close, and did not even announce the marriage to the Court of Vienna; yet she must have foreseen what occurred, namely, that Maria Theresa, mortified not merely in her dignity as a sovereign, but also, and perhaps more, in her ruling passion of benevolent meddlesomeness, would suspend the pension which formed a large portion of the Princess's income, and compel her to the abject apology before restoring it. The marriage with Charles Edward Stuart was worth all that!

Louise of Stolberg was probably well aware of the extreme glory of the marriage for which she had been reserved. The Fitz-Jameses, in virtue of their illegitimate descent from James II, considered themselves and were considered as a sort of Princes of the Blood; and as such they doubtless impressed Louise with a great notion of the glory of the Stuarts, and the absolute legitimacy of their claims. On his marriage Charles Edward assumed the title, and attempted to assume the position, of King of England; so his bride must have considered herself as the wife not merely of the Count of Albany, but of Charles III, King of Great Britain, France, and Ireland. She was going to be a *Queen*! We must try, we democratic creatures of a time when kings and queens may perfectly be adventurers and adventuresses, to put ourselves in the place of this young lady of a century ago, brought up as a dignitary of a chapter into which admission depended entirely upon the number and quality of quarterings of the candidate's escutcheon, under a superior— the Abbess of Ste. Wandru—who was the sister of the late Emperor Francis, the sister-in-law of Maria Theresa; we must try and conceive an institution something between a school, a sisterhood, and a club, in which the ruling idea, the source of all dignity, jealousy, envy, and triumph, was greatness of birth and connection; we must try and do this in order to understand what, to Louise of Stolberg, was the full value of the fact of becoming the wife of Charles Edward Stuart. One hundred and twelve years ago, and seventeen years before the great revolution which yawns, an almost impassable gulf, between us and the men and women of the past, a woman, a girl of nineteen, and a Canoness of Ste. Wandru of Mons, need have been of no base temper if, on the eve of such a wedding as this one, her mind had been full of only one idea: the idea, monotonous and drowningly loud like some big cathedral bell, "I shall be a Queen." But if Louise of Stolberg was, as is most probable, in some such a state of vague exultation, we must remember also that there may well have entered into such exultation an element with which even we, and even the most austerely or snobbishly democratic among us, might fully have sympathised. Her mother, her sister, her brother-in-law, and the old Duke of Fitz-James, who had made up her marriage and married her by proxy, and every other person who had approached her during the last month, must have been filling the mind of Louise of Stolberg with tales of the '45 and of the heroism of Prince Charlie. And her mind, which, as afterwards appeared, was romantic, fascinated by eccentricity and genius, may easily have become enamoured of the bridegroom who awaited her, the last of so brilliant and ill-fated a race, the hero of Gladsmuir and Falkirk, at whose approach the Londoners had shut their shops in terror, and the Hanoverian usurper ordered his yacht to lie ready moored at the Tower steps; the more than royal young man whom (as the Jacobites doubtless told her) only the foolish and traitorous obstinacy of his followers had prevented from reinstating his father on the throne of England. Historical figures, especially those of a heroic sort, remain pictured in men's minds at their moment of glory; and this was the case particularly with the Young Pretender, who had disappeared into well-nigh complete mystery after his wonderful exploits and hairbreadth escapes of the '45; so that in the eyes of Louise of Stolberg the man she was about to marry appeared most probably but little changed from the brilliant youth who had marched on foot at the head of his army towards London, who had held court at Holyrood and roamed in disguise about the Hebrides.

Still, it is difficult to imagine that as the hours of meeting drew nearer, the little Princess, as her travelling carriage toiled up the Apennine valleys, did not feel some terror of the future and the unknown. The spring comes late to those regions; in the middle of April the blackthorn is scarcely budding on the rocks, the violets are still plentiful underneath the leafless roadside hedges; scarcely a faint yellow, more like autumn that spring, is beginning to tinge the scraggy outlines of the poplars, which rise in spectral regiments out of the river beds. Wherever the valley widens, or the road gains some hill-crest, a huge peak white with newly-fallen snow confronts you, closes in the view, bringing bleakness and bitterness curiously home to the feelings. These valleys, torrent-tracks between the steep rocks of livid basalt or bright red sandstone, bare as a bone or thinly clothed with ilex and juniper scrub, are inexpressibly lonely and sad, especially at this time of year.

You feel imprisoned among the rocks in a sort of catacomb open to the sky, where the shadows gather in the early afternoon, and only the light on the snow-peaks and on the high-sailing clouds tells you that the sun is still in the heavens. Villages there seem none; and you may drive for an hour without meeting more than a stray peasant cutting scrub or quarrying gravel on the hill-side, a train of mules carrying charcoal or faggots; the towns are far between, bleak, black, filthy, and such as only to make you feel all the more poignantly the utter desolateness of these mountains. No sadder way of entering Italy can well be imagined than landing at Ancona and crossing through the Apennines to Rome in the early spring. To a girl accustomed to the fat flatness of Flanders, to the market-bustle of a Flemish provincial town, this journey must have been overwhelmingly dreary and dismal. During those long hours dragging up these Apennine valleys, did a shadow fall across the mind of the pretty, fair-haired, brilliant-complexioned little Canoness of Mons, a shadow like the cold melancholy blue which filled the valleys between the sun-smitten peaks? And did it ever occur to her, as the horses were changed in the little post-towns, that it was in honour of Holy Week that the savage-looking bearded men, the big, brawny, madonna-like women had got on their best clothes? Did it strike her that the unplastered church-fronts were draped with black, the streets strewn with laurel and box, as for a funeral, that the bells were silent in their towers? Perhaps not; and yet when, a few years later, the Countess of Albany was already wont to say that her married life had been just such as befitted a woman who had gone to the altar on Good Friday, she must have remembered, and the remembrance must have seemed fraught with ill omen, that last day of her girlhood, travelling through the black deserted valleys of the March, through the world-forgotten mountain-towns with their hushed bells and black-draped churches and funereally strewn streets.

At Loreto—where, as a good Catholic, the Princess Louise of Stolberg doubtless prayed for a blessing on her marriage, in the great sanctuary which encloses with silver and carved marble the little house of the Virgin—at Loreto the bride was met by a Jacobite dignitary, Lord Carlyle, and five servants in the crimson liveries of England. At Macerata, one of the larger towns of the March of Ancona, she was awaited by her bridegroom. A noble family of the province, the Compagnoni-Marefoschis, one of whom, a cardinal, was an old friend of the Stuarts, had placed their palace at the disposal of the royal pair.

We most of us know what such palaces, in small Italian provincial towns south of the Apennines, are apt to be; huge, gloomy, shapeless masses of brickwork and mouldering plaster, something between a mediæval fortress and a convent; great black archways, where the refuse of the house, the filth of the town, has peaceably accumulated (and how much more in those days); magnificent statued staircases given over to the few servants who have replaced the armed bravos of two centuries ago; long suites of rooms, vast, resounding like so many churches, glazed in the last century with tiny squares of bad glass, through which the light comes green and thick as through sea-water; carpets still despised as a new-fangled luxury from France; the walls, not cheerful with eighteenth-century French panel and hangings, but covered with big naked frescoed men and women, or faded arras; few fire-places, but those few enormous, looking like a huge red cavern in the room. The Marefoschis had got together all their best furniture and plate, and the palace was filled with torches and wax lights; a funereal illumination in a funereal place, it must have seemed to the little Princess of Stolberg, fresh from the brilliant nattiness of the Parisian houses of the time of Louis XV.

The bride alighted; a small, plump, well-proportioned, rather childish creature, with still half-formed childish features, a trifle snub, a trifle soulless, very pretty, tender, light-hearted; a charming little creature, very well made to steal folk's hearts unconscious to themselves and to herself.

The bridegroom met her. A faded, but extremely characteristic crayon portrait, the companion of the one of which I have already spoken, now in the possession of Cavaliere Emilio Santarelli (the only man still living who can remember that same Louise d'Albany), a portrait evidently taken at this time, has shown me what that bridegroom must have been. The man who met Louise of Stolberg at Macerata as her husband and master, the man who had once been Bonnie Prince Charlie, was tall, big-boned, gaunt, and prematurely bowed for his age of fifty-two; dressed usually, and doubtless on this occasion, with the blue ribbon and star, in a suit of crimson watered silk, which threw up a red reflection into his red and bloated face. A red face, but of a livid, purplish red suffused all over the heavy furrowed forehead to where it met the white wig, all over the flabby cheeks, hanging in big loose folds upon the short, loose-folded red neck; massive features, but coarsened and drawn; and dull, thick, silent-looking lips, of purplish red scarce redder than the red skin; pale blue eyes tending to a watery greyness, leaden, vague, sad, but with angry streakings of red; something inexpressibly sad, gloomy, helpless, vacant and debased in the whole face: such was the man who awaited Louise of Stolberg in the Compagnoni-Marefoschi palace at Macerata, and who, on Good Friday the 17th of April 1772, wedded her in the palace chapel and signed his name in the register as Charles III, King of Great Britain, France, and Ireland.

II

The Bridegroom

On the Wednesday after Easter the bride and bridegroom made their solemn entry into Rome; the two travelling carriages of the Prince and of the Princess were drawn by six horses; four gala coaches, carrying the attendants of Charles Edward and of his brother the Cardinal Duke of York, followed behind, and the streets were cleared by four outriders dressed in scarlet with the white Stuart cockade. The house to which Louise of Stolberg, now Louise d'Albany, or rather, as she signed herself at this time, Louise R., was conducted after her five days' wedding journey, has passed through several hands since belonging to the Sacchettis, the Muti Papazzurris, and now-a-days to the family of About's charming and unhappy Tolla Ferraldi. Clement XI had given or lent it to the Elder Pretender: James III, as he was styled in Italy, had settled in it about 1719 with his beautiful bride Maria Clementina Sobieska, romantically filched by her Jacobites from the convent at Innsbruck, where the Emperor Charles VI had hoped to restrain her from so compromising a match; here, in the year 1720, Charles Edward had been born and had had his baby fingers kissed by the whole sacred college; and here the so-called King of England had died at last, a melancholy hypochondriac, in 1766. The palace closes in the narrow end of the square of the Santissimi Apostoli, stately and quiet with its various palaces, Colonna, Odescalchi, and whatever else their names, and its pillared church front. There is a certain aristocratic serenity about that square, separated, like a big palace yard, from the bustling Corso in front; yet to me there remains, a tradition of my childhood, a sort of grotesque and horrid suggestiveness connected with this peaceful and princely corner of Rome. For, many years ago, when the square of the Santissimi Apostoli was still periodically strewn with sand that the Pope might not be jolted when his golden coach drove up to the church, and when the names of Charles Edward and his Countess were curiously mixed up in my brain with those of Charles the First and Mary Queen of Scots, there used to be in a little street leading out of the square towards the Colonna Gardens, a dark recess in the blank church-wall, an embrasure, sheltered by a pent-house roof and raised like a stage a few steep steps above the pavement; and in it loomed, strapped to a chair, dark in the shadow, a creature in a long black robe and a skull cap drawn close over his head; a vague, contorted, writhing and gibbering horror, of whose St. Vitus twistings and mouthings we children scarcely ventured to catch a glimpse as we hurried up the narrow street, followed by the bestial cries and moans of the solitary maniac. This weird and grotesque sight, more weird and more grotesque seen through a muddled childish fancy and through the haze of years, has remained associated in my mind with that particular corner of Rome, where, with windows looking down upon that street, upon that blank church-wall with its little black recess, the palace of the Stuarts closes in the narrow end of the square of the Santissimi Apostoli. And now, I cannot help seeing a certain strange appropriateness in the fact that the image of that mouthing and gesticulating half-witted creature should be connected in my mind with the house to which, with pomp of six-horse coaches and scarlet outriders, Charles Edward Stuart conducted his bride.

For the beautiful and brilliant youth who had secretly left that palace twenty-four years before to re-conquer his father's kingdom, the gentle and gallant and chivalric young prince of whose irresistible manner and voice the canny chieftains had vainly bid each other beware when he landed with his handful of friends and called the Highlanders to arms; the patient and heroic exile, singing to his friends when the sea washed over their boat and the Hanoverian soldiers surrounded their cavern or hovel, who had silently given Miss Macdonald that solemn kiss which she treasured for more than fifty years in her strong heart—that Charles Edward Stuart was now a creature not much worthier and not much less repulsive than the poor idiot whom I still see, flinging about his palsied hands and gobbling with his speechless mouth, beneath the windows of the Stuart palace. The taste for drinking, so strange in a man brought up to the age of twenty-three among the proverbially sober Italians, had arisen in Charles Edward, a most excusable ill habit in one continually exposed to wet and cold, frequently sleeping on the damp ground, ill-fed, anxious, worn out by over-exertion in flying before his enemies, during those frightful months after the defeat at Culloden, when, with a price of thirty thousand pounds upon his head, he had lurked in the fastnesses of the Hebrides. We hear that on the eve of his final escape from Scotland, his host, Macdonald of Kingsburgh, prevented the possible miscarriage of all their perilous plans only by smashing the punch-bowl over which the Pretender, already more than half drunk, had insisted upon spending the night. Still more significant is the fact, recorded by Hugh Macdonald of Balshair, that when Charles Edward was concealed in a hovel in the isle of South Uist, the prince and his faithful followers continued drinking (the words are Balshair's own) "for three days and three nights." Hard drinking was, we all know, a necessary accomplishment in the Scotland of those days; and hard drinking, we must all of us admit, may well have been the one comfort and resource of a man undergoing the frightful mental and bodily miseries of those months of lying at bay. But Charles Edward did not relinquish the habit when he was back again in safety and luxury. Strangely compounded of an Englishman and a Pole, the Polish element, the brilliant and light-hearted chivalry, the cheerful and youthfully wayward heroism which he had inherited from the Sobieskis, seemed to constitute the whole of Charles Edward's nature when he was young and, for all his reverses, still hopeful; as he grew older, as deferred and disappointed hopes, and endured ignominy, made him a middle-aged man before his time, then also did the other hereditary strain, the morose obstinacy, the gloomy brutality of James II and of his father begin to appear, and gradually obliterated every trace of what had been the splendour and charm of the Prince Charlie of the '45. Disappointed of the assistance of France, which had egged him to this great enterprise only to leave him shamefully in the lurch, Charles Edward had, immediately upon the peace of Aix la Chapelle, become an embarrassing guest of Louis XV, and a guest of whom the victorious English were continually requiring the ignominious dismissal; until, wearied by the indifference to all hints and orders to free France from his compromising presence, the Court of Versailles had descended to the incredible baseness of having the Prince kidnapped as he was going to the opera, bound hand and foot, carried like a thief to the fortress of Vincennes, and then conducted to the frontier like a suspected though unconvicted swindler, or other public nuisance.

This indignity, coming close upon the irreparable blow dealt to the Jacobite cause by the stupid selfishness which impelled Charles Edward's younger brother to become a Romish priest and a cardinal, appears to have definitively decided the extraordinary change in the character of the Young Pretender. During the many years of skulking, often completely lost to the sight both of Jacobite adherents and of Hanoverian spies, which followed upon that outrage of the year 1748, the few glimpses which we obtain of Charles Edward show us only a precociously aged, brutish and brutal sot, obstinate in disregarding all efforts to restore him to a worthier life, yet not obstinate enough to refuse unnecessary pecuniary aid from the very government and persons by whom he had been so cruelly outraged. We hear that Charles Edward's confessor, with whom, despite his secret abjuration of Catholicism, he continued to associate, was a notorious drunkard; and that the mistress with whom he lived for many years, and whom he even passed off as his wife, was also addicted to drinking; nay, Lord Elcho is said to have witnessed a tipsy squabble between the Young Pretender and Miss Walkenshaw, the lady in question, across the table of a low Paris tavern. The reports of the many spies whom the English Government set everywhere on his traces are constant and unanimous in one item of information: the Prince began to drink early in the morning, and was invariably dead drunk by the evening; nay, some letters of Cardinal York, addressed to an unknown Jacobite, speak of the "nasty bottle, that goes on but too much, and certainly must at last kill him." But, although drunkenness undoubtedly did much to obliterate whatever still remained of the hero of the '45, it was itself only one of the proofs of the strange metamorphosis which had taken place in his character. We cannot admit the plea of some of his biographers, who would save his honour at the price of his reason. Charles Edward was the victim neither of an hereditary vice nor of a mental disease; drink was in his case not a form of madness, but merely the ruling passion of a broken-spirited and degraded nature. He had the power when he married, and even much later in life, when he sent for his illegitimate daughter, of refraining from his usual excesses; his will, impaired though it was, still existed, and what was wanting in the sad second half of his career was not resolution, but conscience, pride, an ideal, anything which might beget the desire of reform. The curious mixture of brow-beating moroseness with a brazen readiness to accept and even extort favours, he would appear, as he ceased to be young, to have gradually inherited from his father; he was ready to live on the alms of the French Court, while never losing an opportunity of declaiming against the ignoble treatment which that same Court had inflicted on him. He became sordid and grasping in money matters, basely begging for money, which he did not require, from those who, like Gustavus III of Sweden, discovered only too late that he was demeaning himself from avarice and not from necessity. While keeping a certain maudlin sentiment about his exploits and those of his followers, which manifested itself in cruelly pathetic scenes when, as in his old age, people talked to him of the Highlands and the Rebellion; he was wholly without any sense of his obligation towards men who had exposed their life and happiness for him, of the duty which bound him to repay their devotion by docility to their advice, by sacrifice of his inclinations, or even by such mere decency of behaviour as would spare them the bitterness of allegiance to a disreputable and foul-mouthed sot. But, until the moment when old and dying, he placed himself in the strong hands of his natural daughter, Charles Edward seems to have been, however obstinate in his favouritism, incapable of any real affection. When his brother Henry became a priest Charles held aloof for long years both from him and from his father; and this resentment of what was after all a mere piece of bigoted folly, may be partially excused by the fact that the identification of his family with Popery had seriously damaged the prospects of Jacobitism. But the lack of all lovingness in his nature is proved beyond possibility of doubt by the brutal manner in which, while obstinately refusing to part with his mistress at the earnest entreaty of his adherents, he explained to their envoy Macnamara that his refusal was due merely to resentment at any attempted interference in his concerns; but that, for the rest, he had not the smallest affection or consideration remaining for the woman they wished to make him relinquish. As if all the stupid selfishness bred of centuries of royalty had accumulated in this man who might be king only through his own and his adherents' magnanimity, Charles Edward seemed, in the second period of his life, to feel as if he had a right over everything, and nobody else had a right over anything; all sense of reciprocity was gone; he would accept devotion, self-sacrifice, generosity, charity—nay, he would even insist upon them; but he would give not one tittle in return; so that, forgetful of the heroism and clemency and high spirit of his earlier days, one might almost think that his indignant answer to Cardinal de Tenein, who offered him England and Scotland if he would cede Ireland to France, "Everything or nothing, Monsieur le Cardinal!" was dictated less by the indignation of an Englishman than by the stubborn graspingness of a Stuart. His further behaviour towards Miss Walkenshaw shows the same indifference to everything except what he considered his own rights. He had crudely admitted that he cared nothing for her, that it was only because his adherents wished her dismissal that he did not pack her off; and subsequently he seems to have given himself so little thought either for his mistress or for his child by her, that, without the benevolence of his brother the Cardinal, they might have starved. But when, after long endurance of his jealousy and brutality, after being watched like a prisoner and beaten like a slave, the wretched woman at length took refuge in a convent, Charles Edward's rage knew no bounds; and he summoned the French Government, despite his old quarrel with it, to kidnap and send back the woman over whom he had no legal rights, and certainly no moral ones, with the obstinacy and violence of a drunken navvy clamouring for the wife whom he has well-nigh done to death. Beyond the mere intemperance and the violence born of intemperance which made Charles Edward's name a byword and served the Hanoverian dynasty better than all the Duke of Cumberland's gibbets, there was at the bottom of the Pretender's character—his second character at least, his character after the year 1750—heartlessness and selfishness, an absence of all ideal and all gratitude, much more morally repulsive than any mere vice, and of which the vice which publicly degraded him was the result much more than the cause. The curse of kingship in an age when royalty had lost all utility, the habit of irresponsibility, of indifference, the habit of always claiming and never giving justice, love, self-sacrifice, all the good things of this world, this curse had lurked, an evil strain, in the nature of this king without a kingdom, and had gradually blighted and made hideous what had seemed an almost heroic character. Royal-souled Charles Edward Stuart had certainly been in his youth; brilliant with all those virtues of endurance, clemency, and affability which the earlier eighteenth century still fondly associated with the divine right of kings; and royal-souled, hard and weak with all the hardness and weakness, the self-indulgence, obstinacy, and thoughtlessness for others of effete races of kings, he had become no less certainly, in the second part of his life; branded with God's own brand of unworthiness, which signifies that a people, or a class, or a family, is doomed to extinction.

Such was the man to whom the easy-going habit of the world, the perfectly self-righteous indifference to a woman's happiness or honour of the well-bred people of that day, gave over as a partner for life a half-educated, worldly-ignorant and absolutely will-less young girl of nineteen and a half, who doubtless considered herself extremely fortunate in being chosen for so brilliant a match.

There is a glamour, even for us, connected with the name of Charles Edward Stuart; in his youth he forms a brilliant speck of romantic light in that dull eighteenth century, a spot of light surrounded by the halo of glory of the devotion which he inspired and the enthusiasm which he left behind him. We feel, in a way, grateful to him almost as we might feel grateful to a clever talker, a beautiful woman, a bright day, as to something pleasing and enlivening to our fancy. But the brilliant effect which has pleased us is like some gorgeous pageant connected with the worship of a stupid and ferocious divinity; nay, rather, if we let our thoughts dwell upon the matter, if we remember how, while the prisons and ship-holds were pestilent with the Jacobite men and women penned up like cattle in obscene promiscuity, while the mutilated corpses were lying still green, piled up under the bog turf of Culloden, while so many of the bravest men of Scotland, who had supplicated the Young Pretender not to tempt them to a hopeless enterprise, were cheerfully mounting the scaffold "for so sweet a prince," Charles Edward was dancing at Versailles in his crimson silk dress and diamonds, with his black-eyed boast the eldest-born Princess of France. Nay, worse, if we remember how the man, for whose love and whose right so much needless agony had been expended, let himself become a disgrace to the very memory of the men who had died for him: if we bear all this in mind, Charles Edward seems to become a mere irresponsible and fated representative of some evil creed; the idol, at first fair-shapen and smiling, then hideous and loathsome, to which human sacrifices are brought in solemnity; a glittering idol of silver, or a foul idol of rotten wood, but without nerves and mind to perceive the weeping all around, the sop of blood at its feet. And now, after the sacrifice of so many hundreds of brave men to this one man, comes the less tragic, less heroic, perfectly legitimate and correct sacrifice to him of a pretty young woman, not brave and not magnanimous, but very fit for innocent enjoyment and very fit for honourable love.

III

Regina Apostolorum

C harles Edward had refrained from drink, or at least refrained from any excesses, in honour of his marriage. Perhaps the notion that France was again taking him up, a notion well-founded since France had bid him marry and have an heir, and the recollection of the near miscarriage of all his projects, thanks to having presented himself, a year before, to the French Minister so drunk that he could neither speak nor be spoken to, perhaps the old hope of becoming after all a real king, had turned the Pretender into a temporarily-reformed character. Or, perhaps, weary of the life of melancholy solitude, of debauched squalor, of the moral pig-stye in which he had been rotting so many years, the idea of decency, of dignity, of society, of a wife and children and friends, may have made him capable of a strong resolution. Perhaps, also, the unfamiliar, wonderful presence of a beautiful and refined young woman, of something to adore, or at least to be jealous and vain of, may have wakened whatever still remained of the gallant and high-spirited Polish nature in this morose and besotten old Stuart. Be this as it may, Charles Edward, however degraded, was able to command himself when he chose, and, for one reason or another, he did choose to command himself and behave like a tolerably decent man and husband during the first few months following on his marriage. Besides the redness of his face, the leaden suffused look of his eyes, the vague air of degradation all about him, there was perhaps nothing, at first, that revealed to Louise, Queen of Great Britain, France, and Ireland, that her husband was a drunkard and well-nigh a maniac. Engaging he certainly could not have been, however much he tried (and we know he tried hard) to show his full delight at having got so charming a little wife; indeed, it is easy to imagine that if anything might inspire even a properly educated and high-born young Flemish or German lady of the eighteenth century with somewhat of a sense of loathing, it must have been the assiduities and endearments of a man such as Charles Edward. But Louise of Stolberg had doubtless absorbed, from her mother, from her older fellow-canonesses, nay, from the very school-girls in the convent where she had been educated, all proper views, negative and positive, on the subject of marriage; nor must we give to a girl who was probably still too much of a child, too much of an unromantic little woman of the world, undeserved pity on account of degradation which she had most probably, as yet, not sufficient moral nerve to appreciate. Her husband was old, he was ugly, he was not attractive; he may have been tiresome and rather loathsome in his constant attendance; he may even have smelt of brandy every now and then; but as marriages had been invented in order to give young women a position in the world, husbands were not expected to be much more than drawbacks to the situation; and as to the sense of life-long dependence upon an individual, as to the desire for love and sympathy, it was still too early in the eighteenth century, and perhaps, also, too early in the life of a half-Flemish, half-German girl, very childish still in aspect, and brought up in the worldly wisdom of a noble chapter of canonesses, to expect anything of that kind.

There must, however, from the very beginning, have been something unreal and uncanny in the girl's situation. The huge old palace, crammed with properties of dead Stuarts and Sobieskis, with its royal throne and daïs in the ante-room, its servants in the royal liveries of England, must have been full of rather lugubrious memories. Here James III of England and VIII of Scotland had moped away his bitter old age; here, years and years ago, Charles Edward's mother, the beautiful and brilliant grand-daughter of John Sobieski, had pined away, bullied and cajoled back from the convent in which she had taken refuge, perpetually outraged by the violence of her husband and the insolence of his mistress; it was an ill-omened sort of place for a bride. Around extended the sombre and squalid Rome of the second half of the eighteenth century, with its huge ostentatious rococo palaces and churches, its straggled, black and filthy streets, its ruins still embedded in nettles and filth, its population seemingly composed only of monks and priests (for all men of the middle-classes wore the black dress and short hair of the clergy), or of half-savage peasants and workmen, bearded creatures, in wonderful embroidered vests and scarves, looking exceedingly like brigands, as Bartolomeo Pinelli etched them even some thirty years later. A town where every doorway was a sewer by day and a possible hiding-place for thieves by night; where no woman durst cross the street alone after dusk, and no man dared to walk home unattended after nine or ten; where, driving about in her gilded state-coach of an afternoon, the Pretender's bride must often have met a knot of people conveying a stabbed man (the average gave more than one assassination per day) to the nearest barber or apothecary, the blood of the murdered man mingling, in the black ooze about the rough cobble-stones over which the coaches jolted, with the blood trickling from the disembowelled sheep hanging, ghastly in their fleeces, from the hooks outside the butchers' and cheesemongers' shops; or returning home at night from the opera, amid the flare of the footmen's torches, must have heard the distant cries of some imprudent person struggling in the hands of marauders; or, again, on Sundays and holidays have been stopped by the crowd gathered round the pillory where some too easy-going husband sat crowned with a paper-cap in a hail-storm of mud and egg-shells and fruit-peelings, round the scaffold where some petty offender was being flogged by the hangman, until the fortunate appearance of a clement cardinal or the rage of the sympathising mob put a stop to the proceedings. Barbarous as we remember the Rome of the Popes, we must imagine it just a hundred times more barbarous, more squalid, picturesque, filthy, and unsafe if we would know what it was a hundred years ago.

But in this barbarous Rome there were things more beautiful and wonderful to a young Flemish lady of the eighteenth century than they could possibly be to us, indifferent and much-cultured creatures of the nineteenth century, who know that most art is corrupt and most music trashy. The private galleries of Rome were then in process of formation; pictures which had hung in dwelling-rooms were being assembled in those beautiful gilded and stuccoed saloons, with their out-look on to the cloisters of a court, or the ilex tops or orange espaliers of a garden, filled with the faint splash of the fountains outside, the spectral silvery chiming of musical clocks, where, unconscious of the thousands of beings who would crowd in there armed with guide-books and opera-glasses in the days to come, only stray foreigners were to be met, foreigners who most likely were daintily embroidered and powdered aristocrats from England or Germany, if they were not men like Winckelmann, or Goethe, or Beckford. It was the great day, also, for excavations; the vast majority of antiques which we now see in Rome having been dug up at that period; and among the ilexes of the Ludovisi and Albani gardens, among the laurels and rough grass of the Vatican hill, porticoes were being built, and long galleries and temple-like places, where a whole people of marble might live among the newly-found mosaics and carved altars and vases. Moreover, there was at that time in Rome a thing of which there is now less in Rome than anywhere, perhaps, in the world—a thing for which English and Germans came expressly to Italy: there was music. A large proportion of the best new operas were always brought out in Rome—always four or five new ones in each season; and the young singers from the conservatorios of Naples came to the ecclesiastical city, where no actresses were suffered, to begin their career in the hoop skirts and stomachers, and powdered *toupés* with which the eighteenth century was wont to conceive the heroines of ancient Greece and Rome. The bride of Charles Edward was herself a tolerable musician, and she had a taste for painting and sculpture which developed into a perfect passion in after life; so, with respect to art, there was plenty to amuse her.

It was different with regard to society. By insisting upon royal honours such as had been enjoyed by his father, but which the Papal Court, anxious to keep on good terms with England, absolutely refused to give him, the Pretender had virtually cut himself and his wife out of all Roman society; for he would not know the nobles on a footing of equality, and they, on the other hand, dared know him on no other. The great entertainments in the palaces where Charles Edward had so often danced, the admired of all beholders, in his boyhood, were not for the Count and Countess of Albany. There remained the theatres and public balls, to which the Pretender conducted his wife with the assiduity of a man immensely vain of having on his arm a woman far too young and too pretty for his deserts. And, besides this, there was a certain amount of vague, shifting foreign society, nobles on the loose, and young men on their grand tour, who mostly considered that a visit to the Palazzo Muti, or at least a seemingly accidental meeting and introduction in the lobby of a theatre or the garden of a villa, was an indispensable part of their sight-seeing. Such people as these were the guests of the Palazzo Muti; and, together with a few Jacobite hangers-on, constituted the fluctuating little Court of Louise, Queen of Great Britain, France, and Ireland, whom the people of Rome, hearing of the throne and daïs in the ante-room and of the royal ceremonial in the palace near the Santissimi Apostoli, usually spoke of as the *Regina Apostolorum*; while only a very few, who had approached that charming little blonde lady, corrected the title to that of Queen of Hearts, Regina dei Cuori. Among the few who bowed before Charles Edward's wife, in consideration of this last-named kingdom, was a brilliant, wayward young man, destined to remain a sort of brilliant, wayward, impracticable child until he was eighty; and destined, also, to cherish throughout the long lives of both, the sort of half genuine, half affected, boy's, or rather page's, passion with which Queen Louise had inspired him. Karl Victor von Bonstetten, of a patrician family of Bern, a Frenchified German, more French, more butterfly-like than any real Frenchman, even of the old *régime*, came to Rome, already well-known by his romantic friendship with the Swiss historian Müller, and by the ideas which he had desultorily and gaily aired on most subjects, in the year 1773. In his memoirs he wrote as follows of the "Queen of Hearts": "She was of middle height, fair, with dark-blue eyes, a slightly turned-up nose, and a dazzling white English complexion. Her expression was gay and *espiègle*, and not without a spice of irony, on the whole more French than German. She was enough to turn all heads. The Pretender was tall, lean, good-natured, talkative. He liked to have opportunities of speaking English, and was given to talking a great deal about his adventures—interesting enough for a visitor, but not equally so for his intimates, who had probably heard those stories a hundred times over. After every sentence almost he would ask, in Italian, 'Do you understand?' His young wife laughed heartily at the story of his dressing up in woman's clothes." A dull, garrulous husband, boring people with stories of which they were sick; a childish little wife, trying to make the best of things, and laughing over the stale old jokes; this is what may be called the idyllic moment in the wedded life of Charles Edward and Louise. What would she have felt, that strong, calm lady, growing old far off in the Isle of Skye, had she been able to see what Bonstetten saw; had she heard the Count and Countess of Albany laughing, the one with the laughter of an old sot, the other with the laughter of a giddy child, over the adventures of that heroic Prince Charlie whose memory was safe in her heart as the sheets he had slept in were safe in her closet, waiting to be her grave-clothes?

Forty-four years later, when the Queen of Hearts was a stout, dowdy old lady, with no traces of beauty, and himself a flighty, amiable old gossip of seventy, Karl Victor von Bonstetten wrote to the Countess of Albany from Rome: "I never pass through the Apostles' square without looking up at that balcony, at that house where I saw you for the first time."

IV

The Heir

In 1765 Horace Walpole, mentioning the now-ascertained fact of the Pretender's abjuration of Catholicism, informed his friend Mann that a rumour was about that Charles Edward had declared his intention of never marrying, in order that no more Stuarts should remain to embroil England. This magnanimous resolution, which was a mere repetition of an answer made years ago by the Pretender's father, did not hold good against the temptations of the Cabinet of Versailles. There is something particularly disgusting in the thought that, merely because the French Government thought it convenient to keep a Stuart in reserve with whom, if necessary, to trip up England, the once magnanimous Charles Edward consented to marry in consideration of a certain pension from Versailles; to make money out of any possible or probable son he might have. This, however, was the plain state of the case; and Louise of Stolberg had been selected, and married to a drunkard old enough to be her father, merely that this honourable bargain between the man outraged in 1748, and the Government which had outraged him, might be satisfactorily fulfilled.

The Court of Versailles wasted its money: the officially-negotiated baby was never born. Nay, Sir Horace Mann, the English Minister at Florence, whose spies watched every movement of the Count and Countess of Albany, was able to report to his Government, in answer to a vague rumour of the coming of an heir, that the wife of Charles Edward Stuart had never, at any moment, had any reasons for expecting to become a mother. And when, in the first years of this century, Henry Benedict, Cardinal York, the younger brother of Charles Edward, was buried where the two melancholy genii of Canova keep watch in St. Peter's, opposite to the portrait of Maria Clementina Sobieska in powder and paint and patches, a certain solemn feeling came over most Englishmen with the thought that the race of James II was now extinct.

But the world had forgotten that the children of Edward IV were resuscitated; that the son of Louis XVI, whose poor little dead body had been handled by the Commissary of the Republic, had returned to earth in the shape of five or six perfectly distinct individuals, Bruneau,

Hervagault, Naundorff, whatever else their names; that King Arthur is still living in the kingdom of Morgan le Fay; and Barbarossa still asleep on the stone table, waiting till the rooks which circle round the Kiefhäuser hill shall tell him to arise; and the world had, therefore, to learn that a Stuart still existed. The legend runs as follows.

In 1773, a certain Dr. Beaton, a staunch Jacobite, who had fought at Culloden, was attracted, while travelling in Italy, by the knowledge that his legitimate sovereigns were spending part of the summer at a villa in the neighbourhood, to a vague place somewhere in the Apennines between Parma and Lucca, distinguished by the extremely un-Tuscan name of St. Rosalie. Here, while walking about "in the deep quiet shades," the doctor was one day startled by a "calash and four, with scarlet liveries," which dashed past him and up an avenue. During the one moment of its rapid passage, the Scotch physician recognised in the rather apocalyptic gentleman wearing the garter and the cross of St. Andrew, who sat by the side of a beautiful young woman, "the Bonnie Prince Charlie of our faithful beau ideal, still the same eagle-featured, royal bird, which I had seen on his own mountains, when he spread his wings towards the south." Towards dusk of that same day, as Dr. Beaton was pacing up and down the convent church of St. Rosalie, doubtless thinking over that "eagle-featured royal bird," whom he had seen driving in the calash and four, he was startled in his meditations by the jingle of spurs on the pavement, and by the approach of a man "of superior appearance."

This person was dressed in a manner which was "a little equivocal," wore a broad hat and a thick moustache, which, joined with the sternness of his pale cheek and the piercingness of his eye, must indeed have suggested something extremely eerie to a well-shaven, three-corner hat, respectable man of the eighteenth century; so that we are not at all surprised to hear that the doctor's imagination was crossed by "a sudden idea of the celebrated Torrifino," who, although his name sounds like a sweetmeat, was probably one of the many mysterious Italians, brothers of the Count of Udolpho and Spalatro and Zeluco, who haunted the readers of the romances of the latter eighteenth century. This personage enquired whether he was addressing "il Dottor Betoni Scozzere."

The physician having answered this question, asked, for no conceivable reason, in bad Italian of a Scotchman by a Scotchman (for we learn that the unknown was a Chevalier Graham), the mysterious moustached man requested him to attend at once upon "one who stood in immediate need." Dr. Beaton's enquiries as to the nature of the assistance and the person who required it, having been answered with the solemn remark that "the relief of the malady, and not the circumstances of the patient, is the province of a physician," and the proposal being made that he should go to the sick person blindfolded and in a shuttered carriage, the doctor's prudence and the thought of the famous Torrifino dictated a flat refusal; but the mysterious stranger would not let him off. "Signor," he exclaimed (persistently talking bad Italian), "I respect your doubts; by one word I could dispel them; but it is a secret which would be embarrassing to the possessor. It concerns the interest and safety of one—the most illustrious and unfortunate of the Scottish Jacobites." "What! Whom?" exclaimed Dr. Beaton. "I can say no more," replied the stranger; "but if you would venture any service for one who was once the dearest to your country and your cause, follow me." "Let us go," cried Dr. Beaton, the enthusiasm for Prince Charlie entirely getting the better of the thought of the famous Torrifino; and so, blindfolded, he was conveyed, partly by land and partly by water (what water, in those Apennine valleys where there are no streams save torrents in which even a punt would be impossible, it is difficult to understand), to a house standing in a garden. That it did stand in a garden appears to have been a piece of information volunteered by the mysterious Chevalier Graham, for Dr. Beaton expressly states that it was not till the two had passed through a "long range of apartments" that the bandage was removed from his eyes.

The doctor found himself in a "splendid saloon, hung with crimson velvet, and blazing with mirrors which reached from the ceiling to the floor. At the farther end a pair of folding doors stood open, and showed the dim perspective of a long conservatory." The mysterious Chevalier Graham rang a silver bell, which summoned a little page dressed in scarlet, with whom he exchanged a few rapid words in German. The communication appeared to agitate the Chevalier; and after dismissing the page, he turned to the doctor. "Signor Dottore," he said, "the most important part of your occasion is past. The lady whom you have been unhappily called to attend, met with an alarming accident in her carriage, not half an hour before I found you in the church, and the unlucky absence of her physician leaves her entirely under your charge. Her accouchement is over, apparently without any result more than exhaustion; but of that you will be the judge."

It was only at the mention of the carriage and the accident that Dr. Beaton, whose wits appear to have been wool-gathering, suddenly guessed at a possible connection between these "most illustrious and unfortunate of Scottish Jacobites," to whose house he had been thus mysteriously introduced, and the lady and gentleman in whom he had that same afternoon recognised Charles Edward and his wife. The page reappeared, and conducted Dr. Beaton through another suite of splendid apartments, till they came to an ante-room decorated with the portraits of no less remarkable persons than the rebel Duke of Perth and King James VIII, a fact which shows that the Stuarts must have carried their furniture with them, from Rome to a Lucchese villa hired for a few months, with more recklessness than one might have imagined likely in those days of post-chaises. Out of this ante-room the physician was ushered into a large and magnificent bed-room, lit with a single taper. From the side of a crimson-draped bed stepped a lady, who saluted Dr. Beaton in English, and led him up to the patient, while a female attendant nursed an infant enveloped in a mantle. The lady drew aside the curtain, and by the faint light the doctor was able to distinguish a pale, delicate face, and a slender white arm and hand lying upon the blue velvet counterpane. The lady in waiting said some words in German, in answer to which the sick woman feebly attempted to stretch out her hand to the physician. Having ascertained that the patient was in a dangerous condition, Dr. Beaton asked for pen and paper to write out a prescription, which, in that Apennine wilderness, would doubtless be made up with the greatest exactness and rapidity. By the side of the writing-desk was a dressing-table; and on what should the doctor's casual glance not rest but a miniature, thrown carelessly among the scent bottles and jewels, and in which he instantly recognised a portrait of Charles Edward such as he had seen him riding on the field of Culloden! But in a moment, when he glanced again from his writing to the toilet-table, the miniature was no longer visible.

The lady having apparently recovered, Dr. Beaton was dismissed, blindfolded as he had come, but only after having taken an oath upon the crucifix "never to speak of what he had heard, or seen, or thought, that night, except it should be in the service of King Charles," and also to quit Tuscany immediately. He repaired, therefore, to the nearest seaport, but was detained there three days before the departure of his ship. One moonlight evening, as he was walking on the sands, he was surprised by seeing an English man-of-war at anchor. In answer to his enquiries, she proved to be the *Albina*, Commodore O'Haloran. While he was lying in a sequestered corner, watching the frigate, he was startled by the sudden appearance of a small closed carriage and of a horseman, in whom, by the moonlight, he immediately recognised the moustached stranger of St. Rosalie. The cavalcade stopped at the water's brink, and the horseman blew a shrill whistle. Immediately a man-of-war's boat shot from behind some rocks and pulled straight towards them. A man with glimmering epaulettes sprang from the boat on to the beach, and helped into it a lady, who had alighted from the carriage, and carried something wrapped in a shawl. Dr. Beaton heard the cry of an infant, the soothing voice of the lady; and, a moment later, after a word and shake of the hand with the moustached man, the boat pulled off from shore. "For more than a quarter of an hour the tall black figure of the cavalier continued fixed upon the same spot, and in the same attitude; but suddenly the broad gigantic shadow of the frigate swung round in the moonshine, her sails filled to the breeze, and dimly brightening in the light, she bore off slow and still and stately towards the west."

Such is the adventure of Dr. Beaton, and thus he is said to have related it, in the year 1831, eighty-five years after the battle of Culloden, where he had himself seen Charles Edward; whence it is presumable that the doctor was considerably over a hundred when he made the disclosure. This story of Doctor Beaton was published, not in a historical work, but in a volume entitled *Tales of the Century; or Sketches of the Romance of History between the years 1746 and 1846*, published at Edinburgh in 1847. But although this book might pass as a work of imagination, and could, therefore, scarcely be impugned as a historical document, there is every reason for supposing that, while not officially claiming to reveal the existence of an heir of the Stuarts, it was deliberately intended to convey information to that effect; and as such, an anonymous writer (either Lockhart or Dennistoun) made short work of it in the *Quarterly Review* for June 1847, from which I have derived the greater part of my knowledge of this curious "romance of history."

Nay, the *Tales of the Century* were undoubtedly intended to insinuate a further remarkable fact: not merely that there still existed heirs of Stuarts in the direct male line, but that these heirs of the Stuarts were no others but the joint authors of the book. The two brothers styling themselves on the title-page John Sobieski Stuart and Charles Edward Stuart, but whose legal names were respectively

John Hay Allan and Charles Stuart Allan, had been known for some years in the Highlands as persons enveloped in a degree of romantic mystery, and claiming to be something much more illustrious than what they were officially supposed to be, the grandsons of an admiral in the service of George III. According to the information collected by Baron von Reumont, the joint authors of the *Tales of the Century* had made themselves conspicuous by their affectation of the Stuart tartan, to which, as Hay Allans, they could have no right; by a certain Stuart make-up (by the help of a Charles I wig which was once found and mistaken for a bird's-nest by an irreverent Highlander) on the part of the elder, and by a habit of bowing to his brother whenever the King's health was drunk on the part of the younger. Moreover the family circumstances of these gentlemen's father coincided exactly with those of the hero of this book, of the supposed son of Charles Edward Stuart and Louise of Stolberg. Their father, Thomas Hay Allan, once a lieutenant in the navy, was known before the law as the younger son of a certain Admiral Carter Allan, who laid claims to the earldom of Errol; and the Jolair Dhearg (for such was the Keltic appellation of the hero of the *Tales of the Century*) was the reputed son of a certain Admiral O'Haloran, who laid claim to the Earldom of Strathgowrie, to which curious parallel the writer in the *Quarterly* adds the additional point that Errol, being in the district of Gowrie, the Earldom of Strathgowrie claimed by the imaginary Admiral O'Haloran was evidently another name for the Earldom of Errol claimed by the real Admiral Carter Allan, two names, by the way, O'Haloran and Carter Allan, of which the first seems intended to reproduce in some measure the sound of the other. The father of Messrs. John Hay and Charles Stuart Allan, was married in 1792, and the hero of the *Tales of the Century* was married somewhere about 1791, both to ladies more suited to the sons of an admiral than to the sons of the Pretender. Taking all these circumstances into consideration it becomes obvious that when the two brothers Hay Allan assumed respectively the names of John Sobieski and Charles Edward Stuart, they distinctly, though unofficially, identified themselves with the sons of the Jolair Dhearg of their book, with the sons of that mysterious infant at whose birth Dr. Beaton had been present, who had been conveyed by night on board the *Albina* and educated as the son of Admiral O'Haloran; in other words, with the sons of the child, unknown to history, of the Count and Countess of Albany.

Now, not only are we assured by Sir Horace Mann, whose spies surrounded the Pretender and his wife, and included even their physicians, that there never was the smallest or briefest expectation of an heir to the Stuarts; but, added to this positive evidence, we have an enormous bulk of even more convincing negative evidence by which it is completely corroborated. This negative evidence consists of a heap of improbabilities and impossibilities, of which even a few will serve to convince the reader. The Pretender married, and was pensioned for marrying, merely that the French Court might have another possible Pretender to use as a weapon against England; is it likely, therefore, that such an heir would be hid away so as to lose his identity, and be completely and utterly forgotten? The Pretender, separated from his wife in consequence of circumstances which will be related further on, called to him, as sole companion of his old age, his illegitimate daughter by Miss Walkenshaw, after neglecting and apparently forgetting both her and her mother for twenty years; is it likely he would have done this had he possessed a legitimate son? Cardinal York assumed the title of Henry IX immediately on the decease of his brother; is it likely that he, always indifferent to royal honours, always faithful to his brother, and now almost dying, would have done so had he known that his brother had left a son? The Countess of Albany, who never relinquished her Stuart position, and who was extremely devoted to children, left her fortune to the painter Fabre; is it likely she would have done so had she been aware that she possessed a child of her own? But there is yet further evidence—I scarcely know whether I should say positive or negative, but in point of fact perhaps both at once, since it is evidence that the word of one, at least, of the joint authors of the *Tales of the Century* cannot outweigh the silence of all other authorities. Five years before the brothers Allan, or Stuart, whichever they should be called, mysteriously informed the world of the adventures of the Jolair Dhearg, the elder of the two, once John Hay Allan, now John Sobieski Stuart, had brought out a magnificent volume, price five guineas, entitled *Vestiarium Scoticum*, and purporting to be a treatise on family tartans written somewhere in the 16th century, and now edited for the first time. The history of this work, as stated in the preface, was well-nigh as complicated and as romantic as the history of the Jolair Dhearg. The only reliable copy of three known by Mr. Sobieski Stuart, of which one was said to exist in the library of the Monastery of St. Augustine at Cadiz, and another had been obtained from an

Edinburgh sword-player and porter named John Ross, was in the possession of the learned editors, and had been given by the fathers of the Scots College at Douay to Prince Edward Stuart, from whom it had, in some unspecified but doubtless extremely romantic manner (probably sewn in the swaddling clothes in which the Jolair Dhearg was consigned to Admiral O'Haloran) descended to Mr. John Sobieski Stuart. This venerable heraldic document appears, if one may judge by the review in the *Quarterly*, to have been well-deserving of publication, owing to the extremely new and unexpected information which it contained upon Scottish archæology. Among such information may be mentioned that it derived several clans from other clans with which they were well known to have no possible connection; that it extended the use of tartans to border-families who had never heard of such a thing; that it contained many words and expressions hitherto entirely unknown in the particular dialect in which it was written; and, moreover, that it multiplied complicated and recondite patterns of tartans in a manner so remarkable that Sir Walter Scott, to whom part of Mr. Sobieski Stuart's transcript of the ancient Ms. was submitted, was led to suspect "that information as to its origin might be obtained even in a less romantic site than the cabin of a Cowgate porter (or the Scots College at Douay), even behind the counter of one of the great clan-tartan warehouses which used to illuminate the principal thoroughfare of Edinburgh."

This important and well-nigh unique document was apparently never submitted in its original Ms. to anyone; the copy from the Scots College at Douay, and the copy from the old sword-player of Cowgate, remained equally unknown to everyone save their fortunate possessor. But transcripts of some portions of the work were submitted, at the request of the Antiquarian Society, to Sir Walter Scott, and as he dismissed the deputation which had met to hear his opinion upon the *Vestiarium Scoticum*, the author of *Waverley* was pleased to remark by way of summing up: "Well, I think the *March* of the next rising" (alluding to the part of the Highlanders in the '45) "must be not 'Hey tuttie tattie,' but 'The Devil among the Tailors.'"

However, perhaps the *Vestiarium Scoticum* may have come out of the Scots College at Douay, and perhaps also the son of Charles Edward Stuart and of Louise of Stolberg may have been born in the room hung with red brocade, and have been handed over to a British Admiral one moonlight night, in the presence of the venerable

Dr. Beaton, whom Providence permitted to attain the unusual age of a hundred years or more, in order that, with unimpaired faculties and unclouded memory, he might transmit to posterity this strange romance of history.

V

Florence

I t is quite impossible to tell the precise moment at which began what Horace Mann, most light-hearted and chirpy of diplomatists, called the Countess of Albany's martyrdom. As we have seen, Charles Edward had momentarily given up all excessive drinking at the time of his marriage. Bonstetten thought him a good-natured garrulous bore, and his wife a merry, childish young woman, who laughed at her husband's oft-told stories. This was the very decent exterior of the Pretender's domestic life in the first year of his marriage. But who can tell what there may have been before beneath the surface? Who can say when Louise d'Albany, hitherto apparently so childish, became suddenly a woman with the first terrible suspicion of the nature of the bondage into which she had been sold? Such things are unromantic, unpoetical, coarse, common-place; yet if the fears and the despair of a guiltless and charming girl have any interest for us, the first whiff of brandy-tainted breath which met the young wife in her husband's embraces, the first qualms and reekings after dinner which came before her eyes, the first bestial and unquiet drunkard's sleep which kept her awake in disgust and terror, these things, vile though they be, are as tragic as any more ideal horrors. At the beginning, most probably, Charles Edward drank only in the evening, and slept off his drunkenness over-night; nor does Bonstetten appear to have guessed that there was any skeleton in the palace at the Santissimi Apostoli. But the spies of the English minister soon reported that Charles Edward was returning to his old ways; that the "nasty bottle," as Cardinal York called it, had got the better of the young wife; and when, two years after their marriage, the Count and Countess of Albany had left Rome and settled in Florence, Charles Edward seems very soon to have acquired in the latter place the dreadful notoriety which he had long enjoyed in the former.

Circumstances also had conduced to replunge the Pretender into the habits to which the renewed hope of political support, the novelty of married life, and perhaps whatever of good may still have been conjured up in his nature by the presence of a beautiful young wife, had momentarily broken through. The French Government, after its sudden pre-occupation about the future of the Stuarts, seemed to have completely forgotten the existence of Charles Edward, except as regarded the payment of the pension granted on his marriage. The child that had been prepaid by that wedding pension, who was to rally the Jacobites round a man whose claims must otherwise devolve legitimately in a few years to the Hanoverian usurpers, the heir was not born, and, as month went by after month, its final coming became less and less likely. Nor was this all. Charles Edward seems to have expected that the sudden interest taken by the Court of Versailles in his affairs, and his new position as a married man and the possible father of a line of Stuarts, would bring the obdurate sovereigns of Italy, and especially the Pope, to grant him those royal honours enjoyed by his father, but hitherto obstinately denied to the moody drunkard whose presence in the paternal palace had been occasionally revealed only by the rumour of some more than ordinarily gross debauch, or the noise of some more than ordinarily violent scene of blackguardly altercation.

Charles Edward, as I have already had occasion to remark, while absolutely callous to the rights which self-sacrifice and heroism might give others over him, was extremely alive to the rights which, as a Stuart and as an obstinate and wilful man, he imagined himself to possess over other folk; and, while it never occurred to him that there might be something slightly ungentlemanly in a prince who had secretly abjured the Catholic faith for political reasons continuing to live in a house and on a pension granted him by the unsuspecting sovereign Pontiff in consideration of his being a martyr for the glory of the Church, he was fully persuaded of the cowardly meanness which prevented Clement XIV, whose interest it was to jog on amicably with England, from acknowledging the grandson of James II as a legitimate King of Great Britain and Ireland. It is therefore easy to conceive the accumulation of disappointment and anger with which Charles Edward saw his hopes deluded. He had, immediately on his return to Rome, officially announced to Clement XIV the arrival in the Eternal City of King Charles III and his Queen, and the Pope had condescended no answer save that he had hitherto been unaware of the existence of such persons, and that he would suffer none such to live under his jurisdiction. He had, for more than a year, imposed upon his wife (despite Cardinal York's and her own entreaties, if we may credit Sir Horace Mann) the title and etiquette of a Queen, and had flaunted his scarlet liveries along the Corso day after day, with no result save that of making the Roman nobles keep carefully out of the way wherever he and his wife might go; nay, more, he had replaced over the doorway of his residence the royal escutcheon of Great Britain, only to return from the country one day and find that the Pontifical police had taken it down during his absence. After this we can understand, as I said, the disappointment and rage which must have accumulated in his heart, and which, fifteen months after his wedding, made him abandon the base town of the popes and seek sympathy and dignity in the capital of Tuscany. But he was destined only to further disappointment. The Grand Duke, Peter Leopold, the practical, economical, priest-hating, paternally-meddlesome, bustlingly and tyrannically-reforming son of Maria Theresa, was not the man to console so mediæval and antiquated and unphilosophical a thing as a Stuart. The arrival, the presence of Charles Edward in Florence, was absolutely ignored by the Court, and no invitations of any sort were sent out either to King Charles III or to the Count of Albany. Except the Corsinis, old friends of the Stuarts, who had known Charles Edward in his brilliant boyhood, and who politely placed at his disposal their half-suburban palace or casino, opening on to the famous Oricellari Gardens, no one seemed inclined to pay any particular respects to the new-comers. There was, indeed, no pressure from the Government (as had been the case in Rome), and the Florentine nobles, whose exclusiveness and pride had been considerably diminished by the inroad of swaggering Lorenese favourites under the Grand Duke Francis, and of cut and dry Austrian officials under his son Peter Leopold, showed a sort of lukewarm willingness to receive the Count and Countess of Albany on equal terms into their society. But Charles Edward wanted royal honours; he forbade his wife demeaning her queenly position by returning the visits of Florentine ladies, and the nobles of the Tuscan Court gradually left the would-be King and Queen of England to their own resources.

These resources, with the exception of receiving such few visitors as might care to know them on unequal terms, and a dogged pushing into notice in every place, promenade, theatre, or nobles' club, where no invitation was required, these resources consisted on the part of Charles Edward in the old, old consoler, the flask of Cyprus or bottle of brandy, in the even grosser pleasures of excessive eating, the indefatigable, assiduous courtship of his young wife, and the occasional rows with his servants and acquaintances. The Count and Countess of Albany appear to have inhabited the Casino Corsini until 1777, when they sent for the greater part of the furniture of their Roman house, and established themselves in a palace, bought of the Guadagnis and later sold to the Duke of San Clemente, between the now suppressed Porta San Sebastiano and the Garden of St. Mark's. In both these places Sir Horace Mann, the vigilant Minister to the Tuscan Court and head spy over the Stuarts in Italy, kept the Pretender well in sight; but, in fact, things had now become so public that spying had grown unnecessary. Already, the year following the removal from Rome to Florence, Sir Horace Mann wrote to Walpole that the Pretender's health was giving way beneath his excesses of eating and drinking; dyspepsia and dropsy were beginning, and a sofa had been ordered for his opera-box, that he might conveniently snooze through the performance. For neither drunkenness nor ailments would induce Charles Edward to let his wife out of his sight for a minute. His systematic jealousy may possibly have originated, as the English Minister reports Charles Edward to have himself declared, from fear lest there might attach to the birth of any possible heir of his those doubts of legitimacy which are almost invariably the lot of a pretender; but there can be no doubt that jealousy was an essential feature of his character, in which it amounted almost to monomania. He had caged his mistress long after he had ceased, by his own avowal, to care for her; he now caged his wife, and with probably about as much or as little affection. He had fenced up Miss Walkenshaw's bed with tables and chairs fitted with bells which the slightest touch set ringing; he now (and so early as 1775) barricaded all avenues to his wife's room excepting the one through his own. Very soon, also, the gross and violent language, the blows which had fallen to the lot of the half-tipsy mistress, were to be shared by the virtuous and patient wife.

For virtuous and patient all accounts unite in showing the young Countess of Albany to have been. In that corrupt Florence of the corrupt eighteenth century, where every married woman was furnished, within two years of her marriage, with an officially appointed lover who sat in her dressing-room while she was finishing her toilet, who accompanied her on all her visits, who attended her to balls and theatres, and, in fact, entirely replaced, by the strict social necessities of the system of cicisbeism, the husband, who was similarly employed about the wife of another; in this society, where conjugal infidelity was a social organisation supplemented by every kind of individual caprice of gallantry; where women were none the worse thought of if they added to the official *cavaliere servente* a whole string of other lovers, varying from the Cardinals of the Holy Church to the singers who played women's parts, in powder and hoops, at the opera; in this world of jog-trot immorality, where jealousy was tolerated in lovers, but ridiculous in husbands, such a couple as the Count and Countess of Albany was indeed a source of pity, wonder, and amazement. But if a husband who barricaded his wife's room, never went out without her, nor permitted her to go out without him, who was never further off than the next room during the presence of any visitor, was a marvellous sight; still more marvellous was a beautiful and charming woman of twenty-three or twenty-four, who cast no glances of longing at the brilliant cavaliers all round her, who consoled her dreary prison-hours with reading hard enough for a professor at the university, and who showed towards the peevish, violent, disgustingly-ailing old toper who overshadowed her life with his presence nothing, as Horace Mann tells us, but attention and tenderness. The fact is that Louise of Stolberg, much as her subsequent life and ways of thought proved her to be a woman of the eighteenth century, and not at all above the eighteenth century's easy-going habits and conventional ideas, was a kind of woman rare at all times and rarest of all in a time like her own, With a kindly and affectionate temper, the immense bulk of her nature, the overbalance, the top-heaviness of it, was intellectual; and intellectual not in the sense of the ready society intelligence, so common among eighteenth-century women, but in the sense of actual engrossing interest and in abstract questions and ideals. The portraits done of her immediately after her marriage show, as I have said, a remarkably childish person; and childish, without much ballast of passion or even likings, the likeness sketched by Bonstetten seems certainly to show her. But there are women who, while immature as women and human beings, are precocious as intellects, and in whom the character, instead of rapidly developing itself by the force of its own emotions and passions, seems in a manner to be called into existence by the intelligence: retarded natures, in whom the thoughts seem to determine the feelings. Of this sort, I think, we must imagine the Countess of Albany, if we would understand the anomalies of her life: a person rather deficient in sensitiveness; indifferent, light-hearted, in her girlhood; not rebelling against the frightful negativeness of existence, the want of love, of youth, of brightness, of all that a young girl can want in the early part of her married life; not rebelling against the positive miseries, the constant presence of everything that was mentally and physically loathsome in the second period of this wedded slavery; a woman of cold temperament, and even, you might say, of cold heart, and safe, safe in the routine of duty and suffering, until a merely intellectual flame burst out, white and cold, in her hitherto callous nature. A creature, so to speak, only half awake, or awake, perhaps, only when she devoured her books and tried to puzzle out her mathematical problems; and going through life by the side of her jealous, brutal, sickly, drunken husband, in a kind of somnambulistic indifferentism, perhaps not feeling her miseries very acutely, and probably not envying other women their meaningless liberty, their inane lovers, their empty wholeness of life.

Thus the routine continued. The Count and Countess of Albany, cured by this time of any affectation of royalty, had gradually got domesticated in Florentine society. People began to go to their house, the newly-bought palace in Via San Sebastiano. People came to the opera-box where Charles Edward lay stretched, dozing or snoring, his bottle of Cyprus wine by his side, on his sofa. It is easy to read through the lines of Sir Horace Mann's pages of social tittle-tattle, that Florence, frivolous and unintellectual and corrupt though it was, and, perhaps, almost in proportion to its frivolity, emptiness, and corruption, felt a strange sort of interest, experienced a vague, mixed feeling, pity, fear, and general surprise and want of comprehension towards this beautiful young woman, with her dazzling white complexion, dark hazel eyes and blonde hair, her childish features grown, perhaps not less young, but more serious and solemn for her five years of wasted youth and endured misery, with her reputation for coldness, her almost legendary eccentricities of intellectual interests. Women like this one are apt to be regarded not so much with dislike and envy, as with the mixed awe and pity which peasants feel towards an idiot, by frivolous and immoral people like those powdered Florentines of a hundred years ago, whose brocaded trains and embroidered coats have long since found their way into the cupboards of curiosity shops, and been cut up into quaint room decoration by æsthetically-minded foreigners; pity and awe the more natural when, as in the case of Louise d'Albany, it is evident to every man and woman, however heartless and stupid, that the creature in question is a victim, and an innocent one. People were led, perhaps to some extent by impertinent curiosity, by the lazy desire to have some opinion to give upon that now legendary household of the besotten, sleepy, nauseous old King of England and his terribly virtuous and intellectual young Queen, to the palace in Via San Sebastiano; and men and women of fashion led thither, as to one of the curious sights of Florence, their country cousins and their distinguished visitors from other parts. And thus, one day in the autumn of 1777, there was brought, we know not by whom, half-curious and half-indifferent, to the *salon* of the Countess of Albany a certain very tall, thin, pale young man of twenty-eight, with handsome, mobile, rather hard aquiline features, choleric, flashing blue eyes, and a head of crisp, bright red hair; a man of fashion, nattily dressed in the Sardinian uniform, but with something strange, untamed, morose about his whole aspect which contrasted singularly with the effete gracefulness and amiability of young Florentine dandies. He had heard of the Countess of Albany's eccentricities long before; she had doubtless heard of his.

One can imagine the curiosity with which the wild, moody young officer fixed those bright, hard, steel, flashing blue eyes upon the beautiful young woman of whom he had heard that she was, what no woman of his acquaintance (and his acquaintance was but too large) had been—intellectual and virtuous. One can imagine the curiosity, much vaguer and more indifferent, with which the woefully cold and woefully weary young woman met the scrutiny of those hard, flashing blue eyes, and took the moral measure of this eccentric creature, come from Turin to Florence with some ten or twelve half-tamed horses, in order to learn Tuscan grammar for the sake of writing tragedies. The common friend, whose name has been engulfed into the unknowable, introduced to the Countess of Albany Count Vittorio Alfieri.

VI

ALFIERI

The childhood and early youth of Vittorio Alfieri had been strangely vacant, dreary, one might almost say intellectually and morally sordid; and the strangest, the dreariest circumstance about them was exactly that this vacuity, this dreariness, this total want of all that can make the life of a boy and of a young man pleasant to our fancy or attractive to our sympathy, did not in the least depend upon any harshness or stinginess of fate. Indeed, perhaps, no man had ever prepared for him an easier existence; no man had ever less misfortune sent to him by Providence, or less unkindness shown towards him by mankind, than this constantly struggling, this pessimistic and misanthropic man. The only son of Count Alfieri of Cortemiglia, of one of the richest and noblest families of Asti in Piedmont, his early childhood was spent under the care of his mother, a woman of almost saintly simplicity and kindness, unworldly, charitable, devoted to her children, and to the poor of the place; and of her third husband, also an Alfieri, who appears to have been, in his affection and generosity towards his wife's children, everything that a step-father is usually supposed not to be. Being delicate in health, the boy was treated with every degree of consideration, never worried with lessons, never exasperated with punishments, as long as he remained at home. He was sent, under the care of an uncle, the eminent architect, Benedetto Alfieri, who appears to have been the ideally amiable uncle as Giacinto Alfieri had been the ideally amiable step-father, to the academy or nobles' college at Turin, where again, provided with plenty of money, and a most accommodating half-tutor, half-valet, he enjoyed, or might have enjoyed, every advantage possible to a young Piedmontese noble, either in the way of study or of idleness. And, finally, when still in his teens, he had been supplied with ample money, horses and fine clothes *ad libitum*, and almost unlimited liberty to wander all over the world, from Naples to Holland, from St. Petersburg to Cadiz, in search of experience or amusement. Nor during those years of youthful wanderings, does he ever seem, except upon one memorable occasion, to have been made to suffer from the unconscientiousness, the harshness, the infidelity, the indifference of the men and women whom he met, any more than in his boyhood he had suffered from the severity of his masters, the brutality of his tutor-servants, or the ill-nature of his fellow pupils. Fate and the world were extremely kind to Vittorio Alfieri: giving him every advantage and comfort, and teaching him no cruel lessons. But Vittorio Alfieri was nevertheless one of the least happy of little boys, and one of the least happy of young men. He was born with an uncomfortable and awkward and unwieldy character, as some men are born lame, or scrofulous, or dyspeptic. The child of a father over sixty, and of a very young mother; there was in him some indefinable imperfection of nature, some jar of character, or some great want, some original sin of mental constitution, which made him different from other men, disabled him from getting pleasure or profit out of the circumstances which gave pleasure or profit to them; and turned his youth into a long period of mental weakness and suffering, from which he recovered, indeed, by a system of moral and intellectual cold water, meagre diet, and excessive exercise, but only to remain for the rest of his days in a condition of character absolutely analogous to the bodily condition of those self-martyring invalids, who keep the gout down by taking exhausting walks, eating next to no dinner, and filling the lives of others with their excitable cantankerousness and gloomy forebodings. There was a numbness and yet a sort of over-sensitiveness about his youth; a strangeness which, without giving the least promise of superior genius, merely made him less happy than other lads.

The word numbness returns to my mind in connexion with this young Alfieri; it certainly does not express the exact impressions left in me by his own narrative of his boyhood and youth, and yet I can find no better word: there was in him something like those irregularities of the circulation due to dyspepsia, which, while making some part of the body, say the head, throb and ache at the least sound, yet leave the whole man dull, heavy, only half-awake.

As a child he had vague and wistful cravings, untempered, unbeautified by such imaginative visions as usually accompany the eccentric feelings of such children as are subject to them. Obstinate and taciturn, he tells us of the curious passion which he experienced for the little choristers, boys of twelve or thirteen, whom he saw serving mass, or heard singing the responses, in the Carmine Church at Asti. Silently, painfully, he seems to have yearned for them in solitude; the daily visit to the church where they shone out in their white surplices, being the only pleasure in this black, blind little life of seven or eight. Some physical ailment, some want of change and movement may have underlain this morbid and sombre passionateness; and we learn that when he was still a tiny boy, having heard that the poisonous hemlock was a sort of grass which brought death, and with no clear notion what death was, but with a vague longing for it, he gorged himself with grass out of the garden, in the belief that there would be some hemlock in it.

At school he learned nothing. The education given at the Academy of Turin may, indeed, have been poor in quantity and quality; still it was the best which a young Piedmontese nobleman could obtain, and Alfieri himself confesses that of his school-fellows most came away with more profit, and some afterwards became cultured and even learned men. He learned nothing because he felt interest, emulation, curiosity about nothing. His nature was still dull, dumb, dormant; and what he calls a period of vegetation might more fitly be termed a moral and intellectual hibernation. His school life is a weary, colourless, featureless part of his autobiography. He would seem to have made neither friends nor enemies. The tricks practised by or upon other school-boys are never mentioned by him; never a practical joke, a lark, a scrape. Of his intellectual tendencies, which were but little developed, we learn only that he exchanged a copy of Ariosto, finally confiscated by the authorities, for a certain number of helpings of chicken, relinquished by him to its possessor; and that he bribed, with eatables also, a certain other boy to tell him stories.

The one incident which sheds light upon the lad's morbid constitution or condition, which reveals that strange, apathetic obstinacy, that *vis inertiæ* which was the spring even of his most decided actions in after life, and which at the same time raises grave doubts in my mind whether there may not have been an actual taint of insanity in this extraordinary being, is the incident of his having submitted, rather than give in after some misdemeanour, to being confined to his room in the Academy for nearly three months at a stretch. Alfieri was fifteen; he might have been let loose for the asking, since there was no real severity in the school. He slept nearly all day long, rose in the evening, but refused to let himself be combed or dressed, and lay for hours on a mattress before the fire, cooking a squalid meal of *polenta* instead of his dinner, which he regularly sent down; receiving the visits of his school-fellows without speaking or even moving; deaf and dumb, as he describes himself, by the hour together, his eyes fixed on the ground, brimful with tears, but never permitting himself to cry or complain—a strange sort of savage animal rather than a human being.

After leaving school at eighteen, he began his long series of journeys, his series of passions for women and for horses, passions dull and dumb, but violent, yet never such as to break through the spell of inarticulateness which seemed to freeze his nature. Nothing more curious can be fancied than his journeys. He went from place to place without being attracted to any, without feeling the smallest interest in anything which he saw, without contracting the faintest attachment for any person or thing, driven along by a sort of fury of restlessness and sombre vacuity. Many youths have doubtless been to the full as indifferent as Vittorio Alfieri to all the objects of interest on their road; but they have been so from frivolity and giddiness, and no one was ever less frivolous or giddy than the young Alfieri. With no particular purity of nature or principles of conduct to restrain him from vice, his dissipation could yet scarcely be called dissipation, so little did it wake up this lethargic, ailing, restless nature. Despite the furious passion which he had for horses, and the hysterical, one might almost say epileptic passions which he experienced for women, he remained characterless, chaotic, only half alive. His many journeys gave him only the negative pleasure of getting away from already known places, the negative wisdom of seeing through a variety of things, military and diplomatic distinctions and national prejudices. He remained joyless and ignorant, and, what was worse, without longing for pleasure or desire for knowledge. More than once kindly men of the world and scholars were smitten with pity for this strange lad, in whom they could not but recognise certain negative qualities rare in the eighteenth century—an intense and cruel truthfulness, an absolute disinterestedness, a constitutional contempt for all the vanities and baseness of the world. They tried to talk to him, to lend him books, to awaken him out of this dormouse sleep of the intellect, to break the spell which weighed him down. All in vain. He continued his life of dull dissipation and dull wanderings, through Italy, Germany, France, England, far into Spain, Portugal, Russia, and even Finland. Periodic fits of depression and of almost sordid avarice showed that he was still the same person as the boy of fifteen who had spent those three months unwashed, unkempt, in savage squalor, by his fireside; and fits of brutal and almost maniac violence, as when, because a hair was sharply pulled out by the roots during the elaborate process of frizzling, he cut open with a blow of a heavy silver candlestick the temple of his faithful valet Elia, who had nursed him like a mother, and whose only revenge, after this fearful scene, was to keep the two handkerchiefs steeped with his blood as a memorial and a warning to his master.

Still, seeing nothing, learning nothing, taking interest in nothing, by turns morosely apathetic and brutally violent, continually intriguing with women, mercenary or depraved, Vittorio Alfieri had, at twenty-five, less things to be proud of, but perhaps less also to regret as absolutely dishonourable, than most young men of his time. He had never lied, never seduced, never stooped to anything which seemed to him demeaning. He was splashed with vice from head to foot, but he was neither unnerved nor warped by it. A subject of constant gossip, of frequent scandal, with his teams of half-tame horses, his flashy clothes, his furious passions for worthless women, his moroseness and violence, he was still, so far, a very negative character, a mere mass of rough material, out of which a man might be made. But who should mould that matter? It is extremely difficult to understand how it came about, as difficult almost as to understand how a certain amount of inorganic molecules will sometimes suddenly seem to obey an impulse from within, and become an organism, a yeast plant, or a microscopic animal; but whether or not we succeed in understanding the how and why of the phenomenon, the phenomenon nevertheless took place; and this unorganised mass of passions called Vittorio Alfieri, this chaotic thing without a higher life or a purpose in the world, only partially sensitive, and seemingly quite impervious to external influence, suddenly obeyed some inner impulse (perhaps some accumulation of unnoticed effects from without), and organised itself into a man, a thinker, and a writer.

Alfieri had always been capable of contempt for others, and largely also of contempt for himself: blind and dull, impulsive and indifferent by turns, he had yet felt acutely the ignominy of certain excesses, whether of avarice, or brutality, or love (if love it may be called), which had ever and anon broken the monotony of his aimless life. Of these ignominies the one he had felt most, perhaps because it deprived him of the independence which even in his stupidest times he put his pride in, was the ignominy of love; that is to say, of what love was to him, unworthy incapacity of doing without a woman whom he despised and even occasionally hated. The very fits of moral hysterics, nay, of moral St. Vitus's dance, of which such love maladies largely consisted, sickened him, degraded him in his own eyes like some disgusting physical infirmity. In his twenty-second year he had such a love malady, he had been the scandal of all London in an intrigue with a certain very lovely Lady Ligonier, who, divorced by her husband for her guilt with the young Italian, was on the point of being joyfully taken to wife by Alfieri when it came out that before being his mistress she had been the mistress of her own groom; a termination of the adventure which, much as it distressed the writer of Alfieri's autobiography, is extremely satisfactory to the reader. A few years later, after a variety of minor love affairs, he became entangled at Turin in the nets of a Marchesa di Prié, a rather faded Armida of very tarnished reputation, and whom he thoroughly despised and even disliked at the very height of his attachment. The struggles between his sense of weariness and degradation and his unworthy love for this woman half wore him out, and brought on a severe malady, from which he recovered only to swear he would never enter her house again, and to return to it as soon as he could stand on his feet. The beautiful social customs of eighteenth-century Italy authorised and even imposed upon a man who had accepted the position of *cavaliere servente* (a sort of pseudo-platonic vice-husbandship which covered illicit connections with a worldly propriety) to attend upon his lady from the moment of her getting up in the morning to the moment when she returned home or dismissed her guests at night, with only a few intervals during which the lover might have his meals or pay his visits; so, when the Marchesa di Prié fell ill of a malady which required absolute repose and silence, Alfieri was bound to spend the whole morning seated at the foot of her bed. During one of these weary watches, it came into his head to kill time by scribbling some dramatic scenes on loose sheets of paper, which he hid during the intervals of his visits under the cushion of an arm-chair. A Piedmontese and a thorough ignoramus, he had scarcely ever attempted to write even so much as a letter in Italian; and as to a literary composition in any language, such a thing had never occurred to him. The *Cleopatra* thus written in his lady's bed-room and secreted under the chair cushion, was a most worthless performance, but it made Alfieri an author. Always devoured by a desire to shine, hitherto by the excellence of his get-up, the beauty of his person, and the number of his horses, it suddenly flashed across him that he might shine in future as a poet. This was the turning-point of his life, or what he called his liberation. But, like a man bound in all his limbs, and who at length has slipped the cord from off one hand, there still remained to Alfieri an infinite amount of struggle, of bitter effort, of hopeless inaction, before he could completely liberate himself from the bonds of sloth, of worldly vanity, dissipation, and unworthy love, before he could step forth and walk steadily along the new road which had appeared to him. His ignorance was appalling. He could no longer construe a line of Latin, he had not for months opened a book; and as to Italian, he knew it no better than any Piedmontese street porter. His idleness, his habit of absolute vacuity, was even worse; his desire to shine before the frivolous women, the inane young men of Turin, nay, merely to have himself, his well-cut coat, his well-frizzled hair, the horse he rode or drove, noticed by any chance loafer in the street, was another almost incredible obstacle; and, worst of all, there was his degrading serfdom to a woman whom he knew he neither loved nor respected, and who had never loved, still less respected, him. But Alfieri, once awakened out of that strange long torpor of his youth, was able to put forth as active and invincible forces all that extraordinary obstinacy, that morose doggedness, that indifference to comfort and pleasure, that brutal violence which had more than once, in their negative condition, made him seem more like some wild animal or half-savage monomaniac than an ordinary young man under five-and-twenty. He had, moreover, at this moment, when all the energies of his nature suddenly burst out, a power of deliberate, complacent, and pitiless moral self-vivisection, a power of performing upon his character such cutting and ripping-open operations as he thought beneficial to himself, which makes one think of the abnormal faculty of enduring pain, the abnormal and almost cruel satisfaction in examining the mechanism of one's own suffering, occasionally displayed by hysterical women; and which brings back the impression already conveyed by the morbid sensitiveness, the frenzied violence, the moody torpor of his youth, that there was something abnormal in Alfieri's whole nature. He was now employing that very hysterical satisfaction in pain and impatience of half measures, to reduce himself, by heroic means, to at least such moral and mental health as would permit the full exercise of his faculties. There exists a diary of his, written in 1777, which is an almost unique example of the seemingly cold, but really excited and hysterical kind of self-vivisection of which I have spoken. Alfieri had always been extraordinarily truthful, not merely for his time and country, but truthful quite beyond the limits of a mere negative virtue. But he was also, what seems almost incompatible with this ferocious truthfulness, excessively self-conscious and morally attitudinising, a thin-skinned *poseur*. To reconcile these seemingly contradictory characteristics, to become what he wished to appear, to pose as what he was, to make himself up (if I may say so) as himself, to intensify what he recognised as his main characteristics and efface all his other ones, now became to Alfieri a sort of unconscious aim of life, closely connected with his avowed desire to become a great poet; "the reason of which desire," he himself wrote in his diary, "is my immoderate ambition, which, finding no other field, has devoted itself entirely to literature." Nothing can be more serious, as I have already remarked, than this diary of Alfieri's struggles, where he notes, day by day, the laziness, the meanness, the want of frankness to himself and others, the despicable vanity, the attempt to appear what he is not, the indulged unfounded suspiciousness towards his friends, all the little base defects which must have pained a nature like his more than any real sinfulness, as the prodding of a surgeon's instruments would have agonised such a man more than an actual amputation. He narrates *in extenso* all his vacillations about nothing at all, all his givings way to laziness, all his insincere confidences made to others. One morning is consumed in debating whether or not he will buy a certain Indian walking-stick: "Torn by avarice and the ambition of having it, I go away without deciding whether I will buy it or not, yet I know full well that before two days are out I shall have bought it. Seeking to understand this contradiction, I discover a thousand ridiculous dirtinesses in my character (*mille ridicole porcherie*)." Another day he notes down, after describing the mean envy with which he has listened to the praises of another member of his little club of dilettante authors: "I do believe that as much praise as is being given and will ever be given to all mankind for every sort of praiseworthy thing, I should like to snap up for myself alone." Again, another day he writes: "More lazy than ever. Walking with a friend, and talking about our incomes, &c. I thought I was giving him a perfectly open account of my money matters; but, with the best intention of telling him the truth, I find that, in order to deceive myself as well as him, I increased my fortune by one-fifth." Again, "I had some doubts whether, as it was blowing hard on the promenade, I would go on as far as where the ladies were walking; because, knowing that I was looking pale and ill, and that the wind had taken the powder out of my hair, I was unwilling to show myself in a condition so unsuitable to my pretensions to beauty."

But while thus analyzing himself, while working at Latin and grammar like a school-boy, this fashionable young man, ashamed of being seen when he was not in good looks, ashamed of having one horse less than usual, was continually ruminating over the glory for which he intended living, and which he appears never for a moment to have doubted of attaining. "In my mind, which is completely given up to the idea of glory, I frequently go over the plan of my life. I determine that at forty-five I will write no more, but merely enjoy the fame which I shall have obtained, or imagine that I have obtained, and prepare myself for death. One thing only makes me uneasy: I fear that as I approach the prescribed limit, I may push it continually back, and that at forty-five I may still be thinking only of continuing to live and, perhaps, of continuing to scribble. Hard as I try to think, or to make others think, that I am different from the rest of mankind, I fear, I tremble lest I be extremely like them."

But in order to devote himself to the pursuit of literary glory, one thing remained to be achieved by this strange, self-conscious, frank, contemptuous, and vain creature, by this young man who, even in his weaknesses, has a certain heroic air about him. It was necessary to break through the bonds of unworthy love. Unable to trust any longer to his often baffled resolution and self-command, Alfieri devised a primitive and theatrical remedy too much in harmony with his whole nature to be otherwise than efficacious. The lady occupied a house in the great rococo square of San Carlo, opposite to the one which he rented; she could not go in or out of her door without being seen by Alfieri, and the sight of her was too much for him: he invariably broke all his resolves and went across the square to his Armida. Knowing this, Alfieri obliged a friend of his to receive from him a solemn written promise to the effect that he would not merely never go to the lady, nor take any notice of her messages, but that, until he felt himself absolutely indifferent and beyond her reach, he would go out only in solitary places and at unlikely hours, and spend the greater part of the day seated at his window looking at her house, seeing her pass, hearing her spoken of, receiving her letters, without ever approaching her or sending her the smallest message. As a pledge of this engagement, Alfieri cut off his long red hair, and sent the plait to his friend, leaving himself in a state of crop-headedness, which made it utterly impossible, in that day when wigs had been given up but short hair had not yet been adopted, for him to appear anywhere. And then he had himself tied to his chair with ropes hidden under his cloak, and spent day after day looking at his mistress' windows, quite unable to read a word or attend to conversation, raging and sobbing and howling like a demoniac, but never asking to be untied; until, at the end of a fortnight or three weeks, he was rewarded, most characteristically, by being at once delivered of all love for his lady, and inspired with the idea for a sonnet.

Alfieri worked harder and harder at his Latin and Italian lessons, sketched out the plan of several plays: and, then, in the early summer of 1776, got together his horses, procured a permission to travel from the King of Sardinia, and set out for Tuscany in order to learn the language in which he was to achieve that great literary glory to which he had dedicated his life.

VII

The Cavaliere Servente

Alfieri's greatest terror in life was to fall in love once more. All his love affairs had been degrading to his good sense, his will and his manhood; they had been odious, even at the moment, to his extraordinary innate passion, or, one might almost say, monomania for independence; he who even in his dullest and most inane years had hated the thought of any sort of military or diplomatic position which should imply subjection to a despotic government, whose only strong feeling about the world in general had long been a fierce hatred and contempt both for those who tyrannised and those who were tyrannised over, this Alfieri had always, as he tells us, fled, though unsuccessfully, from the presence of women whose social position (though the words sound like a sarcasm) was sufficiently good to make any regular love intrigue possible or probable. How much more must he not defend his liberty now that he saw before him the direct road to glory, and felt within himself the power to journey along it.

Thus it was, as he explains in his autobiography, that on his first arrival in Florence, hearing everyone praising the character and talents of the wife of Charles Edward Stuart, and seeing the beautiful young woman at theatres and in the public promenade, he resolutely declined to be introduced to her. The very charm of the impression which she had thus accidentally made upon him, the vivid image of those very dark eyes (I am translating his words, and must explain that her eyes, which seemed blue to Bonstetten and dark to Alfieri's, were in reality of that hazel colour which gives great prominence to the pupil, and therefore leaves the idea of black eyes) contrasting with the brilliant fair skin and pale blonde hair, of the graciousness and sweetness and perhaps even a certain sad austerity in her whole appearance and manner,—all this made Alfieri determine to avoid all personal acquaintance.

But after some months at Siena, where his thoughts had been entirely absorbed in the literary projects which he discussed with his new friend, the grave and good and serious-minded Gori, and one or two Sienese professors, after that first feeling of attraction had died away, and he felt himself covered, as it were, with an impenetrable armour of poetic interests, Alfieri decided, on his return to Florence, that he was quite sufficiently of a new man to expose himself without any danger to such a lady as the Countess of Albany. He was, after all, a different individual from that inane, dull, violent young man who in the vacuity of life had raged and roared in the chains of unworthy love. And she, she also, was quite a different woman from the Lady Ligonier and from the Marchesa di Prié, the shameless, unfaithful wives, and heartless, vain, worldly coquettes who had made such havoc of his heart. She was a cold, virtuous, extremely intellectual woman, trying to find consolation for her quietly and bravely supported miseries in study, in abstract interests which should take away her thoughts from the sickening reality of things; a woman who would be valuable as a friend to a poet, and who would know how to value his friendship. And he, continually seeking for people who could understand his literary ambitions, with whom he could discuss all his poetical projects, and from whom he might receive assistance in this new intellectual life, was he not in need of such a friendship? Would he not appreciate its usefulness and uniqueness sufficiently to see that it did not turn to a mere useless and demoralising love affair? There may also have been something very reassuring to Alfieri's apprehensions in the knowledge that he would be dealing, not with an Italian woman, accustomed and almost socially obliged to hold a man in the degrading bonds of cicisbeism, but with a foreigner, the jealously-guarded wife of a sort of legendary ogre, with whom, however much the old fury of love might awaken in him, there could by no possibility be anything beyond the most strictly watched friendship. So Alfieri went to the palace of the Count of Albany; and, having once been, returned there.

The palace bought by Charles Edward about 1776 stands in the most remote and peaceful quarter of Florence. A few quiet streets, unbroken by shop-fronts and unfrequented by vehicles, lead up to that quarter; streets of low white-washed convent walls overtopped by trees, of silent palaces, of unpretending little houses of the seventeenth or eighteenth century, from behind whose iron window-gratings and blistered green shutters one expects even now, as one passes in the silence of the summer afternoons, to hear the faint jangle of some harpsichord-strummed minuet, the turns and sudden high notes of some long-forgotten song by Cimarosa or Paisiello. It is a region of dead walls, over which bend the acacias and elms, over which shoot up the cypresses and cedars of innumerable convent and palace-gardens, on whose flower-beds and fountains and quincunxes the first-floor windows look down. In the midst of all this, at the corner of two very quiet streets, stands the palace, now of the Duke of San Clemente, an ungainly, yellow structure of various epochs, with a pretty late sixteenth-century belvedere tower on one side; a lot of shuttered and heavily-grated seventeenth-century windows, ornamented with stone stay-laces and tags, upon the dark street; and to the back a desolate old garden, where the vines have crawled over the stonework, and the grotesque seventeenth-century statues, green and yellow with lichen, stand in niches among the ill-trimmed hedges of ilex and laurel: the most old-world house and garden in the old-world part of the town. The eighteenth century still seems very near as we walk in those streets and look in, through the railings, at the ilex and laurel quincunxes, the lichened statues of that garden; and from the roof of the house still floats, creaking in the wind, regardless of the triumph of the Hanoverians, unconscious of the many banners which have been thrown, mere heaps of obsolete coloured tatters, on the dust-heap, a rusty metal weather-vane, bearing the initials of Carolus Rex, the last successor of the standard that was raised in Glenfinnan.

In this house was now developing one of the most singular loves that ever were. Shortly after his introduction to the Countess of Albany, Alfieri, terrified lest he might be forfeiting his spiritual liberty once more, took to flight and tried to forget the lady in a mad journey to Rome. But he had not forgotten her; and on his passage through Siena, returning to Florence, he had explained his feelings, his fears, to his friend Francesco Gori. This Gori, a young Sienese of the middle class, extremely cultured, of "antique uprightness," to use the eighteenth-century phrase, seems to have taken to his heart, as one might some wild younger brother, or some eccentric, moody child, the strange, self-engrossed, passionate Piedmontese. A gentle, grave, and quiet man, he had loved the magnanimity and independence so curiously mingled with mere vanity and egotism in Alfieri's nature; he had never tired of hearing his friend's plans for the future, had never smiled at his almost comic certainty of supreme greatness, he had never lost patience with the self-meritorious egotism which made all Alfieri's actions seem the one interest of the world in Alfieri's own eyes. To Francesco Gori, therefore, Alfieri went for advice: ought he, or ought he not, to fly from this new love while it was still possible to do so?

The grave and virtuous Gori answered that he should not: this new love had been sent to him as a cure for all baser loves; instead of crushing it as an obstacle to his higher life and his glory, he should thankfully cultivate it as an incentive and assistance in working out his intellectual redemption.

Let us pause, and consider for a moment the meaning of Alfieri's question, and the meaning of Gori's answer; let us try and realise the ideas and feelings of two honourable men, seeking a higher life, in a country so near our own as Italy, and so short a while ago as the year 1777. Here was Alfieri, passionately desirous to redeem his own existence by intellectual efforts, and confident of a vague mission to awaken his countrymen to his own nobler feelings: to the contempt of sensual pleasures and worldly vanities, the hatred of political and religious servitude, the love of truth and justice, the love of Italy. Here was this Alfieri, at the very outset of his new career, solemnly confiding to his kindest and wisest friend the scruples, the fears, which restrained him from seeking the company of a woman whom he was beginning to love, and who was beginning to love him, a young woman married by mere worldly convention to a sickly, brutal, and brutish drunkard, old enough to be her father. And what were these scruples? Merely that a new love might distract Alfieri from his plans of study and work, that a woman might cheat him of glory, and Italy of the tragic drama which would school her to virtue. That there could be any other scruples appears never to have crossed Alfieri's brain: that there could be any reason to pause and ask himself whether he was doing wrong or ill before exposing to temptation the woman whom he loved, and the honour which he loved more than her; whether he had a right to return to the palace of Charles Edward and, while receiving his hospitality, while enjoying his confidence, to teach the wife of his host how to love another man than her husband; whether he had a right to return to the presence of that beautiful and intellectual lady, who had hitherto suffered only from the brutishness of her husband, and add to these sufferings the sufferings of hopeless love, the sufferings of a guilty conscience?

But to the Italian of the eighteenth century, even to the man who most thoroughly despised and loathed his country's and century's corruption, no such scruple ever came. What consideration need any man or any woman waste upon a husband? What possible disgrace could come to a woman in having a lover? And did not the frantic jealousy of the besotted old husband, his continual attendance, his perpetual spying, most effectually remove any further consideration there might be for him?

I scarcely know whether it is a thing about which to be cheerful or sad, proud or ashamed; but the more one studies the ideas and feelings of even one's nearest neighbours, in place or in time, the more is one impressed with the sense that, say what people choose, men and women do not think and feel, even upon the most important subjects, in anything like a uniform manner. Social misarrangements, which are crimes towards the individual, are invariably partially righted, made endurable, by individual rearrangements, which are crimes towards society. The woman was not consulted by her parents before her marriage, she was not restrained by her conscience afterwards; she was given for ambition to a man whose tenure of her received legal and religious sanction; she gave herself for love to a man whose possession of her was against society and against religion; but society received her to its parties, and the Church gave her its communion. And thus, in Italy, and in the eighteenth century, where no one had found any fault at a girl of nineteen being married by proxy to a man who turned out to be a disgusting and brutal sot; no one also could find any fault at a young man of twenty-eight seeking, and obtaining, the love of a married woman of twenty-five. The immoral law had produced the immoral lawlessness. So, to the scruples of Alfieri, Francesco Gori had answered: "Return to Florence."

We shall now see how, out of this vile piece of prose, the higher nature of Alfieri and of the Countess of Albany, and (what a satire upon poetic and platonic affection!) most of all, the monomaniac jealousy of Charles Edward, contrived to make a sort of poetry.

VIII

THE ESCAPE

A lfieri's fears had been groundless. His love for the wife of Charles Edward Stuart—a love, he tells us, quite different from any he had previously experienced, quiet, pure, and solemn—was destined not to interfere with that austere process of detaching his soul from the base passions of the world, and devoting it to the creation of a new style of poetry, to the achievement of a new kind of glory; nay, rather, by bringing to the surface whatever capacity for tenderness and self-restraint and respect for others had hitherto lurked within this fantastic nature, this new love helped to complete that strange monumental personality of Alfieri—a personality more striking, more ideal, than any of those plays by which he hoped to regenerate Italy, and which has been far more potent than his works in the moral regeneration of his country. Alfieri's youth had been illiterate and stupid; and he required, in order to make up for so much waste of time and waste of spirit, that he should now be surrounded by an atmosphere as intensely intellectual as the atmosphere in which he had previously lived had been the reverse. After the long spiritual numbness of his earlier years, this soul, if it was to be kept alive, must be kept in an almost artificially high spiritual temperature, and continually plied with spiritual cordials. These advantages he obtained in the love, or, we ought rather to say, the friendship of the Countess of Albany, and it is extremely improbable whether he would have obtained them otherwise. Irritable and vain and moody, at once excessively persuaded of his own dramatic mission and morbidly diffident of his actual powers of carrying it out, contemptuous of others and of himself, Alfieri, who required such constant sympathy and encouragement in his work, was not the man who could hope to obtain much of either from other men, whom his excessive pretensions, his ups and downs of humour, his very dissatisfaction with himself, must have quickly exhausted of the small amount of brotherly tenderness which seems to exist in the literary brotherhood. He did, indeed, meet a degree of sincere helpfulness and friendliness from the members of the Turinese Literary Club; from Cesarotti, the translator of *Ossian*; from Parini, the great Milanese satirist, and from one or two other men of letters; which shows that there is more kindness in the world than he ever would admit, and confirms me in my remark that he was singularly well treated by fate and mankind. But all this was very lukewarm sympathy; and except from his two great friends, Francesco Gori and Tommaso di Caluso, a difficult-tempered man like Alfieri could receive only lukewarmness. Now what he required was sympathy, admiration, adoration, of the most burning description. This was possible, towards such a man, only from a woman. But where find the woman who could give it, among the convent-educated, early corrupted, frivolous ladies of Italy, to whom love-making was the highest interest in life, but an interest only a trifle higher than card-playing, dancing, or dressing? Where, even among the very small number of women like Silvia Verza at Verona, Isabella Albrizzi at Venice, or Paolina Castiglione at Milan, who actually had some amount of culture, and actually prided themselves on it? The rank and file of Italian ladies could give him only another Marchesa di Prié, a little better or a little worse, another woman who would degrade him in the sensual and inane routine of a *cicisbéo*. The exceptional ladies were even worse. Fancy this morbid, conceited, self-doubtful, violent, moody Alfieri accepting literary sympathy in a room full of small provincial lions—sympathy which had to be divided with half a dozen others; learned persons who edited Latin inscriptions, dapper poet priestlets, their pockets crammed with sonnets on ladies' hats, opera-singers, canary birds, births, deaths, and marriages, and ponderous pedants of all sorts and descriptions. Why, a lady who set up as the muse of a hot-tempered and brow-beating creature like Alfieri, a man whom consciousness of imperfect education made horribly sensitive—such a lady would have lost all the accustomed guests of her *salon* in ten days' time. Herein, therefore, consisted the uniqueness of the Countess of Albany, in the fact that she was everything to Alfieri, which no other woman could be. Originally better educated than her Italian contemporaries, the ex-canoness of Mons, half-Flemish, half-German by family, French by training, and connected with England through her marriage with the Pretender, had the advantage of open doors upon several fields of culture. She could read the books of four different nations—a very rare accomplishment in her day; and she was, moreover, one of those women, rarer even in the eighteenth century than now-a-days, whose nature, while unproductive in any particular line, is intensely and almost exclusively intellectual, and in the intellectual domain even more intensely and almost exclusively literary—women who are born readers, to whom a new poem is as great an excitement as a new toilette, a treatise of philosophy (we shall see the Countess devouring Kant long before he had been heard of out of Germany) more exquisitely delightful than a symphony. And this woman, thus educated, with this immense fund of intellectual energy, was living, not a normal life with the normal distracting influences of an endurable husband, of children and society, but a life of frightful mental and moral isolation, by the side, or rather in the loathsome shadow, of a degraded, sordid, violent, and jealous brute, from the reality of whose beastly excesses and bestial fury, of whose vomitings and oaths and outrages and blows, she could take refuge only in the unreal world of books.

With such a woman, Alfieri, accepted as an intimate by the husband, who doubtless thought one hare-brained poet more easy to manage than two or three fashionable gallants—with such a woman as this, Alfieri might talk over plans of self-culture and work, his plays, his essays on liberty and literature, and all the things by which he intended to redeem Italy and make himself immortal, without any fear of his listener ever growing weary; from her he could receive that passionate sympathy and encouragement without which life and work were impossible to him. For we must bear in mind what a man like Alfieri, in the heyday of his youth, his beauty, and that genius which was the indomitable energy and independence of his nature, must have been in the eyes of the Countess of Albany. She had been married at nineteen—she was now twenty-six: in those seven years of suffering there had been ample time to obliterate all traces of the frivolous, worldly girl whom Bonstetten had seen light-heartedly laughing at her old husband's jokes; there had been plenty of time to produce in this excessively intellectual nature that vague dissatisfaction, that desire for the ideal, which is the price too often paid for the consolation of mere abstract and literary interests. The pressure of constant disgust and terror at her husband's doings, the terrible mental and moral solitude of living by such a husband's side, had probably wrought up Louise d'Albany to the very highest and almost morbid refinement of nature—a refinement far surpassing the normal condition of her character, even as the extra fining off of already delicate features by illness will make them surpass by far their healthy degree of beauty. In such a mental condition the sense of what her husband was must have exasperated her imagination quite as much as his actual loathsomeness must have repelled her feelings; the knowledge of the frightful moral and intellectual fall of Charles Edward must have been as bad as the filthy place to which he had fallen. And opposite to the image of the Pretender must constantly have arisen the image of Alfieri—opposite to the image of the man, once heroic and charming and brilliant, who had sold his heroism and his charm, his mind and his manhood, for the bestial pleasure of drink—who had rewarded the devotion and self-sacrifice and noble enthusiasm of his followers by the sight, worse than the scaffold on Tower Hill, of their idol turning into a half-maniac, besotted brute; opposite to this image of degradation must have arisen the image of the man who had wrestled with the baser passions of his nature, who had broken through the base habits of his youth, who had fashioned himself into a noble moral shape as the marble is fashioned by the hand of the sculptor; who was struggling still, not merely with the difficulties of his art, but with whatever he thought mean and slothful in himself.

Some eighteen months after their first acquaintance, Alfieri announced to the wife of Charles Edward that he had just happily settled a most important piece of business, the success of which was one of the most fortunate things of his life. He had made a gift of all his estates to his sister, reserving for himself only a very moderate yearly income; he had reduced himself from comparative wealth to comparative poverty; he had cut himself off from ever making a suitable marriage; he had made himself a pensioner of his sister's husband: but at this price he had bought independence—he was no longer the subject of the King of Sardinia, nor of any sovereign or State in the world.

The passion for political liberty, the abhorrence of any kind of despotism, however glorious or however paternal, had grown in Alfieri with every journey he had made through France, Spain, Germany, Russia—with every sojourn in England; it had grown with every page of Livy and Tacitus, with every line of Dante and Petrarch which he had read; it had grown with every word that he himself had written. He had determined to be the poet who should make men ashamed of being slaves and ashamed of being tyrants. But he was himself the subject of the little military despotism of Piedmont, whose nobles required, every time they wished to travel or live abroad, to beg civilly for leave of absence, which was usually most uncivilly granted; and one of whose laws threatened any person who should print books in foreign countries, and without the permission of the Sardinian censor, with a heavy fine, and, if necessary, with corporal chastisement.

In order to become a poet, Alfieri required to become a free agent; and the only way to become a free agent, to break through the bars of what he called his "abominable native cage," the only way to obtain the power of writing what he wished to write, was to give up all his fortune, and live upon the charity of the relatives whom he had enriched. So, during the past months, he had been in constant correspondence with his sister, his brother-in-law, and his lawyer; and now he had succeeded in ridding himself of all his estates and all his capital. The Countess of Albany knew Alfieri sufficiently well by this time to understand that this alienation of all his property was a real sacrifice. Alfieri was the vainest and most ostentatious of men; young, handsome, showy and eccentric, accustomed to cut a grand figure wherever he went, it must have cost him a twinge to be obliged to reduce his hitherto brilliant establishment, to dismiss nearly all his servants, to sell most of his horses, to exchange his embroidered velvets and satins for a plain black coat for the evening, and a plain blue coat for the afternoon. The worst sacrifice of all he doubtless confided, with savage bitterness, to the Countess, as he confided it to the readers of his autobiography, it was to resign the nominal service of Piedmont—to put aside, for good and all, that brilliant Sardinian uniform in which he looked to such advantage. We can imagine how this subject was talked over—how Alfieri, with that savage pleasure of his in the self-infliction of pain and humiliation, exposed to the Countess all the little, mean motives which had deterred him or which had encouraged him in his liberation from political servitude; we can imagine how she chid him for his rash step, and how, at the same time, she felt a delicious pride in the meanness which he so frankly revealed, in the rashness which she so severely reproved; we can imagine how the thought of Alfieri, who had thus sacrificed fortune, luxury, vanity, to the desire to be free, met in the Countess of Albany's mind the thought of Charles Edward, living the pensioner of a sovereign who had insulted him and of a sovereign whom he had cheated, spending in liquor the money which France had paid him to get himself an heir and the Stuarts another king.

A strange and dangerous situation, but one whose danger was completely neutralised. Of all the various persons who speak of the extraordinary friendship between Vittorio Alfieri and Louise d'Albany which existed at this time, not one even ventures to hint that the relations between them exceeded in the slightest degree the limits of mere passionate friendship; and the solemn words of Alfieri, in whom truthfulness was not merely an essential part of his natural character, but an even more essential part of his self-idealised personality, merely confirm the words of all contemporary writers. Now, if there was a country where an intrigue between a woman noted for her virtue and a poet noted for his eccentricity would, had it existed, have been joyfully laid hold of by gossip, it was certainly this utterly-demoralised Italy of *cavalieri serventi*: every fashionable woman and every fast man would have felt a personal satisfaction in tearing to pieces the reputation of a lady whose whole character and life had been a censure upon theirs. But, as there are women the intensity of whose pure-mindedness, felt in every feature and gesture and word, paralyses even the most ribald wish to shock or outrage, and momentarily drags up towards themselves the very people who would dearly love to drag them down even for a second; so also it would appear that there are situations so strange, meetings of individuals so exceptional, that calumny itself is unable to attack them. No one said a word against Alfieri and the Countess; and Charles Edward himself, jealous as he was of any kind of interference in his concerns, appears never to have attempted to rid himself of his wife's new friend.

Much, of course, must be set down to the very madness of the Pretender's jealousy, to his more than Oriental systematic guarding and watching of his wife. Mann, we must remember, had written, long before Alfieri appeared upon the scene, that Charles Edward never went out without his wife and never let her go out without him; he barricaded her apartment, and was never further off than the next room. Charles Edward undoubtedly conferred upon two people, living in a day of excessive looseness of manners, the inestimable advantage of confining their love within the bounds of friendship, of crushing all that might have been base, of liberating all that could be noble, of turning what might have been merely a passion after the pattern of Rousseau into a passion after the pattern of Dante. But what Charles Edward could not do, what no human being or accidental circumstances could bring about, was due to the special nature of Alfieri and of the Countess; namely, that this strange platonic passion, instead of dying out after a very brief time, merely intensified, became long-lived, inextinguishable, nay continued, in its absolute austerity and purity, long after every obstacle and restraint had been removed, except the obstacles and restraints which, from the very ideality of its own nature, increased for itself. And, if we look facts calmly in the face, and, letting alone all poetical jargon, ask ourselves the plain psychological explanation, we see that such things not only could, but, considering the character of the Countess of Albany and of Alfieri, must have been. The Countess had found in Alfieri the satisfaction of those intellectual and ideal cravings which in a nature like hers, and in a situation like hers, must have been the strongest and most durable necessities. Alfieri, on the other hand, sick of his past life, mortally afraid of falling once more under the tyranny of his baser nature, seeking on all sides assistance in that terrible struggle of the winged intellect out of the caterpillar cocoon in which it had lain torpid so long, was wrought up, if ever a man was, to the pitch of enjoying, of desiring a mere intellectual passion just in proportion as it was absolutely and completely intellectual.

A poet especially in his conception of his own personality, an artist who manipulated his own nature, a *poseur* whose *pose* was his concentrated self cleared of all things which recalled the vulgar herd; moreover, a furiously literary temper with a mad devotion to Dante and Petrarch: Alfieri must have found in this love, which fate in the Pretender's person ordained to be platonic, the crowning characteristic of his present personality, the almost miraculous confirmation of his mystic relationship to the lover of Beatrice and the lover of Laura. And, in the knowledge of what he was to this poor, tormented young wife; in the consciousness of being the only ray of light in this close-shuttered prison—nay, rather bedlam-like existence; in the sense of how completely the happiness of Louise d'Albany depended upon him, whatever there was of generous and dutiful in the selfish and self-willed nature of Alfieri must have become paramount, and enjoined upon him never to vacillate or grow weary in this strange mixture of love and of friendship.

IX

ROME

This strange intellectual passion, the meeting, as it were, of two long-repressed, long solitary intellectual lives, austerely satisfied with itself and contemptuous of all baser loves, might have sufficed for the happiness of two such over-wrought natures as were at that moment Vittorio Alfieri and Louise d'Albany.

But there could be no happiness for the wife of the Pretender, and no happiness, therefore, for the man who saw her the daily victim of the cantankerousness, the grossness and the violence of her drunken husband. To an imaginative mind, loving in things rather the ideal than the reality, striving for ever after some poetical or heroic model of love and of life, trying to be at once a patriot out of Plutarch and a lover after the fashion of the *Vita Nuova*, there are few trials more exasperating than to have to see the real creature who for the moment embodies one's ideal, the creature whom one carefully garlands with flowers and hangs round with lamps, raised above all vulgar things in the niche in one's imagination, elbowed by brutish reality, bespattered with ignoble miseries. And this Alfieri had constantly to bear. Perhaps the very knowledge of the actual suffering, of the unjust recriminations, the cruel violence, the absolute fear of death, among which Louise d'Albany spent her life, was not so difficult for her lover to bear as to see her, the beautiful and high-minded lady of his heart, seated in her opera box near the sofa where the red and tumid-faced Pretender lay snoring, waking up, as Mann describes him, only to summon his lacqueys to assist him in a fit of drunken sickness, or to be carried, like a dead swine, with hanging bloated head and powerless arms, downstairs to his carriage; not so difficult to bear as to hear her, his Beatrice, his Laura, made the continual victim of her bullying husband's childish bad-temper, of his foul-mouthed abuse, to hear it and have to sit by in silence, dependent upon the good graces of a besotted ruffian against whom Alfieri's hands must have continually itched.

A little poem, poor, like all Alfieri's lyrics, written about this time, and complaining of having to see a beautiful pure rose dragged through ignoble filth, shows that Alfieri, like most poetical minds, resented the vulgar and the disgusting much more than he would have resented what one may call clean tragedy. But things got worse and worse, and the real tragedy threatened. Charles Edward had outraged and beaten his mistress; older and much more profoundly degraded, he now outraged and beat his wife. In 1780 Sir Horace Mann reports upon the "cruel and indecent behaviour" of which Mme. d'Albany was the victim. Ill-treatment and terror were beginning to undermine her health, and there can be no doubt, I think, that the symptoms of a nervous disorder, of which she complained a couple of years later to Alfieri's bosom friend Gori, must originally have been produced in this unusually robust young woman by the horrible treatment to which she was at this time subjected. Mme. d'Albany, who had astonished the world by her resignation, appears to have fairly taken fright; she wrote to her brother-in-law Cardinal York, entreating him to protect her from her husband. The weak-minded, conscientious cardinal was not the man to take any bold step; he promised his sister-in-law all possible assistance if she were driven to extremities, but begged her to endure a little longer and save him the pain of a scandal. So the Countess of Albany, long since abandoned by her own kith and kin, abandoned also by her brother-in-law, alone in the world between a husband who was daily becoming more and more of a wild beast, and a lover who was fearful of giving any advice which might compromise her reputation or separate them for ever, went on suffering.

But the moment came when she could suffer no more. At the beginning of the winter of 1780, the celebration of St. Andrew's day by Charles Edward and his drinking companions, was followed by a scene over which Alfieri drops a modest veil, calling it vaguely a violent bacchanal which endangered the life of his lady. From the biographers of Charles Edward we learn that the Pretender roused his wife in the middle of the night with a torrent of insulting language which provoked her to vehement recriminations; that he beat her, committed foul acts upon her, and finished off with attempting to choke her in her bed, in which he would probably have succeeded had the servants not been waked by the Countess's screams and dragged Charles Edward away.

Alfieri, partly from an honourable reluctance to see his lady made the heroine of a public scandal, and partly, no doubt, from the more selfish fear lest a separation from her husband might imply a separation also from her lover, had long persisted in advising the Countess against any extreme measure. Alfieri tells us that with the desire for freedom of speech and writing at the bottom of his act of self-spoliation in his sister's favour, there had mingled a sense also that by breaking all connections with Piedmont, and liberating himself from all temptation of marrying for the sake of his family, he was, in a manner, securing the continuation of his relations with Mme. d'Albany. The Countess's flight from her husband, they both well knew, would in all probability put an end to these relations; the Catholic Church could grant no divorce, and Charles Edward would probably refuse a separation; so that the honour, nay, the life of the fugitive wife would be safe only in a convent, whence Alfieri would be excluded together with Charles Edward. The choice was a hard one to make; the choice between a life of peace and safety, but separated from all that made life dear to her, and a life consoled by the presence of Alfieri, but made wretched and absolutely endangered by the violence of a drunken maniac. But after that frightful night of St. Andrew no choice remained; to remain under the Pretender's roof was equivalent for his wife either to a violent death in another such fit of madness, or to a lingering death from sheer misery and daily terror. The Countess of Albany must leave her husband.

To effectuate this was the work of Alfieri—of Alfieri, who, of all men, was most interested to keep Mme. d'Albany in her husband's house; of Alfieri, who, of all men, was the least fitted for any kind of underhand practices. The actual plot for escape was the least part of the business; the conspiracy would have utterly miscarried, and Mme. d'Albany have been condemned to a life of much worse agony, had not provision been made against the Pretender's certain efforts to get his wife back. Mme. d'Albany may have remembered how her mother-in-law Clementina Sobieska, although protected by the Pope, had been eventually got out of the convent whither she had escaped, and had been restored to her husband the Pretender James; she was probably aware, also, how Charles Edward had stormed at the French Government to have Miss Walkenshaw sent back to him from the convent at Meaux. No Government could give a man back his mistress, but it was different with a wife; and both Alfieri and the Countess must have known full well that however lax the Grand Ducal Court might be on the subject of conjugal infidelity, when quietly carried on under the domestic roof and dignified by the name of *serventismo*, no court, no society, could do otherwise than virtuously resent so great a turpitude as a wife publicly running away by herself from her husband's house. It became necessary to win over the sympathies of those in power, to secure their connivance, or at all events their neutrality; and this task of talking, flattering, wheedling, imploring, fell to Alfieri, whose sense of self-debasement appears to have been mitigated only by the knowledge that he was working for the good of a guiltless and miserable woman, of the woman whom he loved more than the whole world; by the bitter knowledge that the success of his efforts, the liberation of his beloved, meant also the sacrifice of that intercourse which made the happiness of his life.

Alfieri succeeded; the Grand Duke and the Grand Duchess were won over. The actual flight alone remained to be accomplished.

In the first days of December 1780 a certain Mme. Orlandini, a half Irish lady connected with the Jacobite Ormonds, was invited to breakfast at the palace in the Via San Sebastiano. She skilfully led the conversation into a discussion on needle-work, and suggested that the Countess of Albany should go and see the last embroidery produced at the convent of Bianchette, a now long-suppressed establishment in the adjoining Via del Mandorlo. The Countess of Albany ordered her carriage for immediately after breakfast, and the two ladies drove off, accompanied, of course, by Charles Edward, who never permitted his wife to go out without him. Near the convent-gate they met a Mr. Gahagan, an Irish Jacobite and the official *cavaliere servente* of Mme. Orlandini, who, hearing that they were going to pay a visit to the nuns, offered to accompany them. Gahagan helped out the Countess and Mme. Orlandini, who rapidly ran up the flight of steps leading to the convent door; he then offered his arm to Charles Edward, whose legs were disabled by dropsy. Leaning on Gahagan's arm, the Pretender was slowly making his way up the steps when his companion, looking up, suddenly exclaimed that the two ladies had already entered the convent and that the nuns had stupidly and rudely shut the door in his and the Count of Albany's face. "They will soon have to open," answered Charles Edward, and began to knock violently. Mr. Gahagan doubtless knocked also. But no answer came. At length the door opened, and there appeared behind a grating no less a person than the Lady Abbess, who ceremoniously informed the Count that she was unable to let him in, as his wife had sought an asylum in her convent under the protection of Her Highness the Grand Duchess of Tuscany.

Sir Horace Mann says that Alfieri, who is not mentioned in the very circumstantial narrative of Dutens, was hanging about the convent, in order to prevent the Pretender, who always carried pistols in his pockets, from committing any violence. This seems extremely unlikely, as the first use to which Charles Edward would naturally have put his pistols would have been shooting Alfieri, for whose murder he immediately offered a thousand sequins. At any rate, raging like a maniac, the discomfited husband went back to his empty house.

It would be pretty and pathetic to insert in this part of my narrative a page of half-condemnatory condolence with Charles Edward. But this I find it perfectly impossible to do. Of course, if we call to mind Falkirk and Skye, if we conjure up in our fancy the Prince Charlie who still lived in the thoughts of Flora MacDonald, there is something very frightful in this tragi-comic flight of the Countess of Albany: the slamming of that convent door in his face is the worst injury, the worst injustice, the worst ignominy reserved by fate for the last of the unhappy Stuarts.

But of the Charles Edward of the Forty-five there remained so little in this Count of Albany that we have no right to consider them any longer as one individual, to condone the brutishness of the Count of Albany for the sake of the chivalry of Prince Charles, to degrade our conception of the young man by tacking on to it the just ignominy inflicted upon the old man, the man who had inherited his name and position, but scarcely his personality. Above all, we have no right to add to whatever reproaches we may think fit to shower upon the Countess of Albany and on Alfieri, the imaginary reproach that the husband whose rights they were violating was the victor of Gladsmuir and Falkirk.

There must always be something which shocks us in the behaviour, however otherwise innocent and decorous, of a woman who runs away from her husband with the assistance of her lover; but this quality of offensiveness is not, in such a case as the present one, a fault of the woman: it is one of her undeserved misfortunes, as much as is the bad treatment, the solitude, the temptation, to which she has been subjected. The evil practice of the world, its folly and wickedness in permitting that a girl like Louise of Stolberg should be married to a man like Charles Edward, its injustice and cruelty in forbidding the legal breaking of such an unrighteous contract; the evil practice of the world which condemned the Countess of Albany to be for so much of her life an unhappy woman, also condemned her to be in some of her actions a woman deserving of blame. We shall see further on how, in the attempt to work out their happiness in despite of the evil world in which they lived, the Countess and Alfieri, infinitely intellectually and morally superior to many of us whom circumstances permit to live blameless and comfortable, were splashed with the mud of unrighteousness, which was foreign to their nature, and remained spotted in the eyes of posterity.

Charles Edward did what he had done once before in his life: he applied to the Government to put him again in possession of the woman whom he had victimised; but as the French Government had refused to recognise his claims over his fugitive mistress, so the Government of the Grand Duke of Tuscany now refused to give him back his fugitive wife. The Countess of Albany had naturally taken no clothes with her in her flight; and she presently sent a maid to the palace in Via San Sebastiano to fetch such things as she might require. But Charles Edward would not permit a single one of her effects to be touched; if she wanted her clothes and trinkets, she might come and fetch them herself. However, after a few days, a message came from the Pope, ordering the Pretender to supply his wife with whatever she might require; a threat to suspend the pension was probably expressed or implied, for Charles Edward immediately obeyed.

Meanwhile, the Countess of Albany was anxiously awaiting at the convent of the Bianchette a decision from her brother-in-law, to whom she had written immediately after her flight. Those first days must have been painfully unquiet. What if the Tuscan Court should listen to the Count of Albany's entreaties? What if Cardinal York should take part with his brother? Return to the house of her husband would be death or worse than death. Cardinal York answered immediately: a long, kind, rather weak-minded letter, the ideal letter of a well-intentioned, rather silly priest, in curious Anglo-Roman French. He informed her that for some time past he had expected to hear of her flight from her husband; he protested that he had had no hand in her unhappy marriage, and begged her to believe that it had been out of his power to protect her. He had informed the Pope of the whole affair, and with His Holiness' approval had prepared for his sister-in-law a temporary asylum in the Ursuline convent in Rome, whither he invited her to remove as soon as possible. In January 1781 the Countess of Albany, accompanied by a Mme. de Marzan, who appears to have formed part of her household, and two maids, started for Rome; but such had been the threats of Charles Edward, and his ravings to get his wife back, that Alfieri and Gahagan, armed and dressed as servants, accompanied the carriage a considerable part of its way. The Pretender, we must remember, had offered a thousand sequins to anyone who would kill Alfieri; and even in that humdrum late eighteenth century a man of position might easily hire a couple of ruffians to waylay a carriage and kidnap a woman.

The Countess of Albany was installed in the Ursuline convent in Via Vittoria, a street near the Piazza di Spagna. A gloomy family memory hung about the place: it had been the asylum of Clementina Sobieska when she had fled from the elder Pretender as Louise d'Albany had fled from the younger. But the wife of Charles Edward was in a very different mood from the wife of James III and it is probable that, despite the many charms of the convent, and the excellent manners of its aristocratic inmates, upon which Cardinal York had laid great store, the Countess, with her heart full of the thought of Alfieri, was not at all inclined to give her pious brother-in-law the satisfaction, which he apparently expected, of developing a sudden vocation for Heaven.

She had left Florence at the end of the year; in the spring she saw Alfieri again. The quiet work which had seemed so natural and easy while he was sure of seeing his lady every day, had become quite impossible to him. He felt that he ought to remain in Florence, that he ought not to follow her to Rome. But Florence had become insufferable to him; and he determined to remove to Naples, because to get to Naples it was necessary to pass through Rome. The melancholy barren approach to the Eternal City, which, three years before, had inspired Alfieri with nothing but melancholy and disgust, now seemed to him a sort of earthly paradise; and Rome, which he hated, as the most delightful of places. He hurried to the Ursuline convent, and was admitted to speak to the Countess of Albany. "I saw her," he wrote many years later, "but (O God! my heart seems to break at the mere recollection) I saw her a prisoner behind a grating; less tormented than in Florence, but yet not less unhappy. We were separated, and who could tell how long our separation might not last? But, while crying, I tried to console myself with the thought that she might at least recover her health, that she would breathe freely, and sleep peacefully, no longer trembling at every moment before the indivisible shadow of her drunken husband; that she might, in short, live."

X

Antigone

About three months after the Countess of Albany's flight from her husband, the Pope granted her permission to leave the Ursuline convent; and her brother-in-law, Cardinal York, offered her hospitality in his magnificent palace of the Cancelleria. Alfieri was at Naples when he received this news, riding gloomily along the sea-shore, weeping profusely (for we must remember that to an Italian, especially of the eighteenth century, there is no incongruity in a would-be ancient Roman shedding love-sick tears), unable to give his attention to work, living, as he expresses it, on the coming in and going out of the post. "I wished to return to Rome," he writes, "and at the same time I felt very keenly that I ought not to do it yet. The struggles between love and duty which take place in an honourable and tender heart, are the most terrible and mortal pain that a man can suffer. I delayed throughout April, and I determined to drag on through May; but on the 12th May I found myself, I scarcely know how, back in Rome."

Alfieri found the Countess of Albany established in the palace of the Cancelleria, the mistress of the establishment, for her brother-in-law was living in his episcopal town of Frascati. They were free to see each other as much as they chose, to love each other as much as they would; for the Cardinal and the priestly circles seem to have gone completely to sleep in the presence of this critical situation; and the habits of Roman society, which were even a shade worse than those of Florence, were not such as to give umbrage to the lovers. But those years during which they had loved under the vigilant jealousy of Charles Edward, had apparently fostered a love which was accustomed and satisfied with being only a more passionate kind of friendship; the indomitable power of resistance to himself, the passion for realising in himself some heroic attitude which he admired, and the almost furious desire to reverse completely his former habits of life, kept Alfieri up to the point of a platonic connexion; and the Countess of Albany, intellectual, cold, passive, easily moulded by a more vehement nature, loved Alfieri much more with the head than with the heart, and loved in him just that which made him prefer that they should meet and love as austerely as

Petrarch and Laura. The fact was, I believe, that the Countess of Albany had much more mind than personality, and that she was therefore mere wax in the hands of a man who had become so exclusively and violently intellectual as Alfieri: she had seen too much of the coarse realities of life, of the brutal giving way to sensual impulse: the heroic, the ideal, nay the deliberately made up, the artificial, had a charm for her. Be this as it may, the Countess and Alfieri continued, in the opinion of all contemporaries, and according to the assurance of Alfieri himself, whose cynicism and truthfulness are equal, on the same footing as in Florence.

And these months in Rome seem to have been the happiest months of Alfieri's life, the happiest, probably, of the life of the Countess of Albany. Alfieri hired the villa Strozzi, on the Esquiline, a small palace built by one of Michel Angelo's pupils, and for which, including the use of furniture, stables, and garden, he paid the now incredibly small sum of ten scudi a month, about two pounds of our money. Permitting himself only two coats, the black one for the evening, and the famous blue one for ordinary occasions, and limiting his dinner to one dish of meat and vegetables, without wine or coffee, Alfieri contrived to make the comparatively small pension paid to him by his sister, go almost as far as had the fine fortune of which he had despoiled himself. He spent lavishly on books, and more lavishly on horses, on horses which, according to his own account, were his third passion, coming only after his love for Mme. d'Albany, and sometimes usurping the place of his love of literary glory.

The mania for systematic division of his time, the invincible tendency to routine, which follows in most Italians after the disorder and wastefulness of youth, had already got the better of Alfieri. He had, almost at the moment when the passion for literature first disclosed itself, made up his mind to write a definite number of tragedies, first twelve, then fourteen, and no more; and to devote a certain number of years to the elaborate process of first constructing them mentally, then of writing them full length in prose, and finally of turning this prose into verse; and he was later to devise a corresponding plan of writing an equally fixed number of comedies and satires in an equally fixed number of years, after which, as we have seen, he was to give up his thoughts, having attained the age of forty-five, to preparing for death.

This routine is a national characteristic, and absorbs many an Italian, turning all the poetry of his nature to prose, with a kind of dreadful inevitableness; but Alfieri did not merely submit to routine, he enjoyed it, he devised and carried it out with all the ferocity of his nature. To this man, who cared so much for the figure he cut, and so little for all the things which surrounded him, a life reduced to absolute monotony of grinding work was almost an object of æsthetic pleasure, almost an object of sensual delight: he enjoyed a dead level, an endless white-washed wall, as much as other men, and especially other poets, enjoy the ups and downs, the irregularities and mottled colours of existence. So Alfieri arranged for himself, in his house near Santa Maria Maggiore, what to him was a life of exquisite delightfulness.

He spent the whole early morning reading the Latin and Italian classics, and grinding away at his tragedies, which, after repeated sketching out, repeated writing out in prose, were now going through the most elaborate process of writing, re-writing, revising, and re-revising in verse. Then, before resuming his solitary studies in the afternoon, he would have one of his many horses saddled, and ride about in the desolate tracts of the town, which in papal times extended from Santa Maria Maggiore to the Porta Pia, the Porta San Lorenzo, and St. John Lateran: miles of former villa gardens, with quincunxes and flower-beds, cut up for cabbage-growing, wide open spaces where the wall of a temple, the arch of an aqueduct, rose crowned with wall-flower and weeds out of the rank grass, the briars and nettles, the heaps of broken masonry and plaster, among which shone beneath the darting lizards, scraps of vermilion wall-fresco, the chips of purple porphyry or dark-green serpentine; long avenues of trees early sere, closed in by arum-fringed walls, or by ditches where the withered reeds creaked beneath the festoons of clematis and wild vine; solemn and solitary wildernesses within the city walls, where the silence was broken only by the lowing of the herds driven along by the shaggy herdsman on his shaggy horse, by the long-drawn, guttural chant of the carter stretched on the top of his cart, and the jingle of his horse's bells; places inaccessible to the present, a border-land of the past, and which, as Alfieri says, thinking of those many times when he must have reined in his horse, and vaguely and wistfully looked out on to the green desolation islanded with ruins and traversed by the vast procession of the aqueducts, invited one to meditate, and cry, and be a poet. And sometimes—we know it from the sonnets to his horse Fido, who had, Alfieri tells us, carried the beloved burden of his lady—Alfieri did not ride out alone. One of the horses of the villa Strozzi was saddled for the Countess of Albany; and this strange pair of platonic lovers rode forth together among the ruins, the wife of Charles Edward listening, with something more than mere abstract interest, to Alfieri's fiercest contemptuous tirades against the tyranny of soldiers and priests, the tyranny of sloth and lust which had turned these spots into a wilderness, and which had left the world, as Alfieri always felt, and a man not unlike Alfieri in savage and destructive austerity, St. Just, was later to say, empty since the days of the Romans.

Towards dusk Alfieri put by his books, and descended through the twilit streets of the upper city—where the troops of red and yellow and blue seminarists, and black and brown monks, passed by like ants, homeward bound after their evening walk—into the busier parts of Rome, and crossing the Corso filled with painted and gilded coaches, and making his way through the many squares where the people gathered round the lemonade-booth near the fountain or the obelisk, through the tortuous black streets filled with the noise of the anvils and hammers of the locksmiths and nailors behind the Pantheon, made his way towards the palace, grand and prim in its architecture of Bramants, of the Cancelleria, perhaps not without thinking that in the big square before its windows, where the vegetable carts were unloaded every morning, and the quacks and dentists and pedlars bawled all day, a man as strange, as wayward and impatient of tyranny as himself, Giordano Bruno, had been burned two centuries before by Cardinal York's predecessor in that big palace of the Cancelleria. Fortunately there was no Cardinal York in the Cancelleria, or at least only rarely; but instead only the beautiful blonde woman with the dark hazel eyes, whom Alfieri spoke of as his "lady," and, somewhat later, "as the sweet half of himself," and in whose speech Alfieri was never Alfieri, or Vittorio, or the Count, but merely "the poet," so completely had these strange, self-modelling, unconsciously-attitudinising lovers, arrayed themselves and their love according to the pattern of Dante and Petrarch.

To the Countess, we may be sure, Alfieri never failed to give a most elaborate account of his day's work, nor to read to her whatever scenes of his plays he had blocked out, in prose, or worked up in verse. By 11 o'clock, he tells us, he was always back in his solitary little villa on the Esquiline.

But this, although it is probably correct with regard to his visits to Mme. d'Albany, with whom consideration for gossip prevented his staying much after ten at night, must not be taken as the invariable rule; for Alfieri, devoted as he was to his lady, by no means neglected other society. He was finishing his allotted number of tragedies, and, as the solemn moment of publication approached, he began to be tormented with that same desire to display his work to others, to hear their praises even if false, to understand their opinion even if unfavourable, which came, by gusts, as one of the passions of his life. Rome was at that time, like every Italian town, full of literary academies, conventicles of very small intellectual fry meeting in private drawing-rooms or at coffee-houses, and swayed by the overlordship of the famous Arcadia, which had now sunk into being a huge club to which every creature who scribbled, or daubed, or strummed, or had a coach-and-pair, or a bad tongue, or a pretty face, or a title, belonged without further claims. There were also several houses of women who affected intelligence or culture, having no claims to beauty or fashion; and foremost among these, but differing from them by the real originality and culture of the lady of the house, the charm of her young daughter, and the superior quality of the conversation and music to be enjoyed there, was the house of a Signora Maria Pizzelli, of all women in Rome the one to whom, after the Countess of Albany, Alfieri showed himself most assiduous. In her house and in many others Alfieri began to give almost public readings of his plays; trying to persuade himself that his object in so doing was to judge, from the expression of face and even more from the restlessness or quiescence of his listeners on their chairs, how his work might affect the mixed audience of a theatre; but admitting in his heart of hearts that the old desire to be remarked had as much to do with these exhibitions as with the six-horse gallops which used to astonish the people of Turin and Florence.

But something better soon offered itself. The Duke Grimaldi had had a small theatre constructed in the Spanish palace, his residence as Ambassador from the Catholic King, and a small company of high-born amateurs had been playing in it translations of French comedies and tragedies. To these ladies and gentlemen Alfieri offered his *Antigone*, which was accepted with fervour. The beautiful and majestic Duchess of Zagarolo was to act the part of the heroine; her brother and sister-in-law, the Duke and Duchess of Ceri, respectively the parts of Hæmon and of Argia, while the character of Creon, the villain of the piece, was reserved for Alfieri himself. The performance of *Antigone* was a great solemnity. The magnificent rooms of the Spanish Embassy were crowded with the fashionable world of Rome, which, in the year 1782, included priests and princes of the Church quite as much as painted ladies and powdered cavaliers. A contemporary diary, kept by the page of the Princess Colonna, a certain Abate Benedetti, enables us to form some notion of the assembly. Foremost among the ladies were the two rival beauties, equally famous for their conquests in the ecclesiastical as well as the secular nobility, the Princess Santacroce and the Princess Altieri, vying with each other in the magnificence of their diamonds and of their lace, and each upon the arm of a prince of the Church who had the honour of being her orthodox *cavaliere servente*; the Princess Altieri led in by Cardinal Giovan Francesco Albani, the very gallant and art-loving nephew of Winckelmann's Cardinal Alessandro; the Princess Santacroce escorted by the French Ambassador Cardinal de Bernis, the amiable society rhymester of Mme. de Pompadour, whom Frederick the Great had surnamed *Babet la bouquetière*. In the front row sat the wife of the Senator Rezzonico, who, in virtue of being the niece of the late Pope Clement XIII, affected an almost royal pomp, and by her side sat the wittiest and most literary of the Sacred College, the still very flirtatious old Cardinal Gerdil. The hall was nearly full when the stir in the crowd, and the general looking in one direction, announced the arrival of a guest who excited unwonted attention. A young woman, who scarcely looked her full age of thirty, small, slender, very simply and elegantly dressed, with something still girlish in her small irregular features and complexion of northern brilliancy, was conducted along the gangway between the rows of chairs, and, as if she were the queen of the entertainment, solemnly installed by the side of the Princess Rezzonico in the first row. Was it because her husband had called himself King of England, or because her lover was the author of the play about to be performed? Be it as it may, the Countess of Albany was the object of universal curiosity, and the emotion which she displayed during the play was a second and perhaps more interesting performance for the scandal-loving Romans.

While the ghosts of these long dead men and women, ladies in voluminous brocaded skirts and diamond-covered bosoms, bursting out of the lace and jewels of their stiff bodices, cardinals in trailing scarlet robes and bishops with well-powdered hair contrasting curiously with their Dominican or Franciscan dress, Roman nobles all in the strange old-world costumes, with ruffs and trunk hose and emblazoned mantles, of the Pope's household and of the military orders of Malta and Calatrava, secular dandies in elaborately-embroidered silk coats and waistcoats, ecclesiastical dandies to the full as dapper with their heavy lace, and abundant fob jewels and inevitable two watches on the sober black of their clothes;—while these ghosts whom we have evoked in all their finery (long since gone to the *bric-à-brac* shops) to fill the theatre-hall of the Spanish palace, sit and listen to the symphony which Cimarosa himself has written for *Antigone*, sit and watch the magnificent Duchess of Zagarolo, dressed as Antigone in hoop and stomacher and piled-up feathered hair, and the red-haired eccentric Piedmontese Count, the d'Albany's lover, bellowing the anger of Creon; let us try and sum up what the tragedies of Alfieri are for us people of today, and what they must have been for those people of a hundred years ago.

While scribbling for mere pastime at his earliest play, Alfieri had felt his mind illumined by a sort of double revelation: he would make his name immortal, and he would create a new kind of tragedy. These two halves of a proposition, of which he appears never to have entertained a single moment's doubt, had originated at the same time and developed in close connection: that he could be otherwise than an innovator was as inconceivable to Alfieri as that he could be otherwise than a genius, although, in reality, he was as far from being the one as from being the other. The fact was that Alfieri felt in himself the power of inventing a style and of producing works which should answer to the requirements of his own nature: considering himself as the sole audience, he considered himself as the unique playwright. Excessively limited in his mental vision, and excessively strong in his mental muscle, it was with his works as with his life: the ideal was so comparatively within reach, and the will was so powerful, that one feels certain that he nearly always succeeded in behaving in the way of which he approved, and in writing in the style which he admired. And the most extraordinary part of the coincidence was, that as he happened to live in a time and country which had entirely neglected the tragic stage, and consequently had no habits or aspirations connected with it, his own desires with reference to Italian tragedy preceded those of his fellow-countrymen, his own ideal was thrust upon them before they well knew where they were; and his own nature and likings became the sole standard by which he measured his works, his own satisfaction the only criterion by which they could be judged. In order, therefore, to understand the nature of Alfieri's plays, it is necessary, first of all, to understand what were Alfieri's innate likings and dislikings in the domain of the drama. Before all other things, Alfieri was not a poet: he lacked all, or very nearly all, the faculties which are really poetical. To begin with the more gross and external ones, he had no instinct for, no pleasure in, metrical arrangements for their own sake; he did not think nor invent in verse, ideas did not come to him on the wave of metre; he thought out, he elaborately finished, every sentence in prose, and then translated that prose into verse, as he might have translated (and in some instances actually did translate) from a French version into an Italian one. Moreover he was, to a degree which would have been surprising even in a prose writer, deficient in that which constitutes the intellectual essence of poetry as metre constitutes its material externality; in that tendency to see things surrounded by, disguised in, a swarm, a masquerade, of associated ideas; deficient in the power of suggesting images, of conceiving figures of speech; in fancy, imagination, in the metaphorical faculty, or whatever else we may choose to call it. Nor did he perceive or describe visible things, visible effects, in their own unmetaphorical shapes and colours: not a line of description, not an adjective can be found in his works except such as may be absolutely indispensable for topographical or similar intelligibility; Alfieri obviously cared as little for beautiful sights as for beautiful sound. This being the case, everything that we might call distinctly poetical, all those things which are precious to us in Shakespeare, or Marlowe, or Webster, in Goethe or Schiller, nay, even, occurring at intervals, in Racine himself, at least as much as mere psychology or oratory or pathos, appeared to Alfieri in the light of mere meretricious gewgaws, which took away from the interest of dramatic action without affording him any satisfaction in return. As it was with metre and metaphor and description, so it was also with the indefinable something which we call lyric quality: the something which sings to our soul, and which sends a thrill of delight through our nerves or a gust of emotion across our nature in the same direct way as do the notes of certain voices, the phrases of certain pieces of music: instantaneously, unreasoningly and unerringly. Of this Alfieri had little, so little that we may also say that he had nothing; the presence of this quality being evidently unnoticed by him and unappreciated. So much for the absolutely poetical qualities. Of what I may call the prose qualities of a playwright, only a certain number appealed to Alfieri, and only a certain number were possessed by him. In a time when the novel was beginning to become a psychological study more minute than any stage play could ever be, Alfieri was only very moderately interested in the subtle analysis or representation of character and state of mind; the fine touches which bring home a person or a situation did not attract his attention; nor was he troubled by considerations concerning the probability of a given word or words being spoken at a particular moment and by a particular man or woman: realism had no meaning for him. As it was with intellectual conception, so was it also with instructive sympathy: Alfieri never subtly analysed the anatomy of individual nature, nor did he unconsciously mimic its action and tones; what most of us mean by pathos did not appeal to him. Neither metrical nor imaginative pleasurableness, nor descriptive charm, nor lyric poignancy, nor psychological analysis or intention entered, therefore, into Alfieri's conception of a desirable tragedy, any more than any of these things fell within the range of his special talents; for, we must always bear in mind that with this man, whose feelings and desires were in such constant action and reaction, with this man whose will imposed his intellectual notions on his feelings, and his emotional tendencies on his thoughts, the thing which he enjoys is always as the concave to the convex of the thing which he produces. But although Alfieri was not a poet, and was not even a potential novel writer, he was, in a sense, essentially a dramatist; though even here we must distinguish and diminish. Alfieri was not a man who cared for rapid action or for intricate plot: he never felt the smallest inclination to violate the old traditions of the pseudo-classic stage by those thrilling scenes or sights which had to be described and not shown, nor by those complications of interest which require years for an action instead of the orthodox twenty-four hours.

He was perfectly satisfied with the no-place, no-where—with the vague temple, or palace hall, or public square where, as in the country of the abstract, the action of pseudo-classic tragedy always takes place, or, more properly speaking, the talking of pseudo-classic tragedy always goes on; he was perfectly satisfied with sending in a servant or a messenger to inform the public of a murder or suicide committed behind the scenes; he was perfectly satisfied with taking up a story, so to speak, at the eleventh hour, without tracing it to its original causes or developing it through its various phases. In such matters Alfieri was as undramatic as Corneille or Racine. Nevertheless Alfieri had a distinct dramatic sense: an intense *poseur* himself, enjoying nothing so much as working himself up to produce a given effect upon his own mind or upon others, he had an extraordinary instinct for the theatrical, for the moral attitude which may be struck so as to be effective, and for the arrangement of subordinate parts so that this attitude surprise and move the audience. The moral attitude, the psychological gesture, which thus became the main interest of Alfieri's plays, was, as might be expected from such a man, nearly always his own moral attitude, his own psychological gesture; he himself, his uncompromising, unhesitating, unflinching, curt and emphatic nature, is always the hero or heroine of the play, however much the situation, the incidents, the other characteristics may vary. Antigone is generous and tender, Creon is inhuman in all save paternal feeling, Saul is a suspicious madman, Agamemnon a just and confiding hero, Clytæmnestra is sinful and self-sophisticating, Virginia pure and open-minded; yet all these different people, despite all their differences, speak and act as Alfieri would speak and act, could he, without losing his peculiar characteristics, adopt for the moment vices or virtues which would become quite secondary matters by the side of his essential qualities of pride, narrowness, decision, violence, and self-importance. Whether he paint his face into a smile or a scowl, whether he put on the blond wig of innocence, or the black wig of villainy, the man's movement and gesture, the tone of his voice, the accent of his words, the length of his sentences, are always the same: so much so that in one play there may be two or three Alfieris, good and bad, Alfieris turned perfectly virtuous or perfectly vicious; but anything that is not an Alfieri in some tolerably transparent disguise, is sure to be a puppet, a lay figure with as few joints as possible, just able to stretch out its arms and clap them to its sides, but dangling suspended between heaven and earth.

The attitude and the gesture, which are the things for whose sake the play exists, are, as I have said, the attitude and gesture of Alfieri. But the moral attitude and gesture of Alfieri happened to be just those which were rarest in the eighteenth century in all countries, and more especially rare in Italy; and they were the moral attitude and gesture which the eighteenth century absolutely required to become the nineteenth, and which the Italy of Peter Leopold and Pius VI and Metastasio and Goldoni absolutely required to become the Italy of Mazzini and Garibaldi, the Italy of Foscolo and Leopardi: they were the attitude and the gesture of single-mindedness, haughtiness, indifference to one's own comfort and one's neighbours' opinion, the attitude and gesture of manliness, of strength, if you will, of heroism. To have written tragedies whose whole value depended upon the striking exhibition of these qualities; and to have made this exhibition interesting, nay, fascinating to the very people, to the amiable, humane, indifferent, lying, feeble-spirited Italians of the latter eighteenth century, till these very men were ashamed of what they had hitherto been; to stamp the new generation with the clear-cut die of his own strong character; this was the reality of the mission which Alfieri had felt within himself: a reality which will be remembered when his plays shall have long ceased to be acted, and shall long have ceased to be read. Alfieri imagined himself to be a great poetic genius, and a great dramatic innovator: he scorned with loathing the works of Corneille, of Racine, and of Voltaire, all immeasurably more valuable as poetry and drama than his own; he hated the works of Metastasio, a poet and a playwright by the divine right of genius; he refused to read Shakespeare, lest Shakespeare should spoil the perfection of his own conceptions. He slaved for months and years perfecting each of his plays, recasting the action and curtailing the dialogue and polishing the verse; yet the action was always heavy, the dialogue unnatural to the last degree, the verse unpoetical. But all this extraordinary self-sufficiency was not a delusion, all this extraordinary labour was not a waste: Alfieri, who never had a single poetical thought, nor a single art-revolutionising notion, was yet a great genius and a great innovator, inasmuch as he first moulded in his own image the Italian patriot of the nineteenth century. His use consisted in his mere existence among men so different from himself; and his dramas, his elaborately constructed and curtailed and corrected dramas, were, so to speak, a system of mirrors by which the image of this strange new-fangled personality might be flashed everywhere into the souls of his contemporaries. To perceive the moral attitude and gesture specially characteristic of himself, to artificially correct and improve and isolate them in his own reality, and then to multiply their likeness for all the world; to know himself to be Alfieri, to make himself up as Alfieri, and to write plays whereof the heroes and heroines were mere repetitions of Alfieri; such was the mission of this powerful and spontaneous nature, of this self-conscious and self-manipulating *poseur*.

The success of that performance of *Antigone* on the amateur stage in the Spanish palace was very great. A young man, half lay, half ecclesiastic, a dubious sort of poet, secretary, factotum, accustomed to write not the most sincere poetry, and to execute, perhaps, not the most creditable errands, of the Pope's dubious nephew, Duke Braschi—a young man named Vincenzo Monti, was present at this performance, or one of the succeeding ones; and from that moment became the author of the revolutionary tragedy of *Aristodemo*, the potential author of that famous ode on the battle of Marengo, one of the forerunners of new Italy. Nay, even when, some few months later, there died at Vienna the old Abate Metastasio, and his death brought home to a rather forgetful world what a poet and what a dramatist that old Metastasio had been; even then, an intimate friend of the dead man, a worldly priest, a quasi prelate, the Abate Taruffi, could find no better winding up for the funeral oration, delivered before all the pedants and prigs and fops and spies of pontifical Rome assembled in the rooms of the Arcadian academy, than to point to Count Vittorio Alfieri, and prophesy that Metastasio had found a successor greater than himself.

XI

Separation

Alfieri and the Countess were happy, happier, perhaps, than at any other time of their lives; but this happiness had to be paid for. The false position in which, however faultlessly, they were placed; the illegitimate affection in which, however blamelessly, they were indulging; these things, offensive to social institutions, although in no manner wrong in themselves, had produced their fruit of humiliation, nay, of degradation. Fate is more of a Conservative than we are apt to think; it resents the efforts of any individual, be he as blameless as possible, to resist for his own comfort and satisfaction the uncomfortable and unsatisfactory arrangements of the world; it punishes the man who seeks to elude an unjust law by condemning him to the same moral police depôt, to the same moral prison-food, as the villain who has eluded the holiest law that was ever framed; and Fate, therefore, soiled the poetic passion of Alfieri and his lady by forcing it to the base practices of any illicit love. The manner in which Fate executes these summary lynchings of people's honour could not usually be more ingenious; there seems to be a special arrangement by which offenders are punished in their most sensitive part. The punishment of Alfieri and of Mme. d'Albany for refusing to sacrifice their happiness to the proprieties of a society which married girls of nineteen to drunkards whom they had never seen, but which would not hear of divorce; this punishment, falling directly only upon the man, but probably just as heavy upon the woman who witnessed the humiliation of the person whom she most loved and respected, consisted in turning Alfieri, the man who was training Italy to be self-respecting, truthful, unflinching, into a toady, a liar, and an intriguer.

The Countess of Albany, living in the palace of her brother-in-law, Cardinal York, and under the special protection of the Pope, was entirely dependent on the good pleasure of the priestly bureaucracy of the Rome of Pius VI, that is to say, of about the most contemptible and vilest set of fools and hypocrites and sinners that can well be conceived; the Papacy, just before the Revolution, had become one of the most corrupt of the many corrupt Governments of the day. Cardinal York himself was a weak and silly, but honest and kind-hearted man; but Cardinal York was entirely swayed by the prelates and priests and priestlets and semi-priestly semi-lay nondescripts among whom he lived. He was responsible for the honour of the Countess of Albany, that is to say, of her husband and his brother; and the honour of the Countess of Albany depended exactly upon the remarks which the most depraved and hypocritical clergy in Europe, the people who did or abetted all the dirty work of Pius VI and his Sacred College, chose to make or not to make about her conduct.

Such were the persons upon whom depended the liberty and happiness of Alfieri's lady, the possibility of that high-flown Platonic intercourse which constituted Louis d'Albany's whole happiness, and Alfieri's strongest incentive to glory; a word from them could exile Alfieri and lock the Countess up in a convent. The consequence of this state of things is humiliating to relate, since it shows to what baseness the most high-minded among us may be forced to degrade themselves. Already, during those few days' sojourn in Rome, before his stay in Naples and Mme. d'Albany's release from the Ursuline convent, Alfieri had spent his time running about flattering and wheedling the powers in command (that is to say, the corrupt ministers of the Papacy and their retinue of minions and spies), in order to obtain leave to inhabit the same city as his beloved and to see her from time to time; doing everything, and stooping to everything, he tells us, in order to be tolerated by those priests and priestlets whom he abhorred and despised from the bottom of his heart. "After so many frenzies, and efforts to make myself a free man," he writes, in his autobiography, "I found myself suddenly transformed into a man paying calls, and making bows and fine speeches in Rome, exactly like a candidate on promotion in prelatedom." At this price of bitter humiliation, nay, of something more real than mere humiliation, Alfieri bought the privilege of frequenting the palace of Cardinal York. But it was a privilege for which you could not pay once and for all; its price was a black-mail of humbugging, and wheedling, and dirt-eating.

Alfieri hated and despised all sovereigns and all priests; and if there were a sovereign and a priest whom he despised and hated more than the rest, it was the then reigning Pius VI, a vain, avaricious, weak-minded man, stickling not in the least at humiliating Catholicism before anyone who asked him to do it, by no means clean-handed in his efforts to enrich his family, without courage, or fidelity to his promise; a man whose miserable end as the brutally-treated captive of the French Republic has not been sufficient to raise to the dignity of a martyr. Of this Pope Pius VI did Alfieri crave an audience, and to him did he offer the dedication of one of his plays; nay, the man who had sacrificed his fortune in order to free himself from the comparatively clean-handed despotism of Sardinia, who had stubbornly refused to be presented to Frederick the Great and Catherine II, who had declined making Metastasio's acquaintance on account of a too deferential bow which he had seen the old poet make to Maria Theresa; the man who had in his portfolios plays and sonnets and essays intended to teach the world contempt for kings and priests, this man, this Alfieri, submitted to having his cheek patted by Pope Braschi. This stain of baseness and hypocrisy with which, as he says, he contaminated himself, ate like a hidden and shameful sore into Alfieri's soul; yet, until the moment of writing his autobiography, he had not the courage to display this galling thing of the past even to his most intimate friends. To Louise d'Albany, to the woman between whom and himself he boasted that there was never the slightest reticence or deceit, he screwed up the force to tell the tale of that interview only some time later. Alfieri, honest enough to lay bare his own self-degradation, was not generous enough to hide the fact that this self-degradation was incurred out of love for her. That her hero should have stooped so low, so low that he scarcely dared to tell even her, surely this must have been as galling to the Countess of Albany as was the caress of Pius VI to Alfieri himself; this high poetic love of theirs, this exotic Dantesque passion, had been dragged down, by the impartial legality of fate, to the humiliating punishment which awaited all the basest love intrigues in this base Rome of the base eighteenth century.

And, after some time, the stock of toleration bought at the price of this baseness was exhausted. The clerical friends and advisers of Cardinal York, who had hitherto assured the foolish prince of the Church that he was acting for the honour of his brother and his brother's wife in leaving a young woman of thirty-one to the sole care of a young poet of thirty-four, each being well known to be over head and ears in love with the other; these prudent ecclesiastics, little by little, began to change their minds, and the success of Alfieri's plays, the general interest in him and his lady which that success produced, suggested to them that there really might be some impropriety in the familiarity between the wife of Charles Edward and the author of *Antigone*. The train was laid, and the match was soon applied. In April 1783 the Pretender fell ill in Florence, so ill that his brother was summoned at once to what seemed his death-bed. Charles Edward recovered. But during that illness the offended husband, who, we must remember, had offered a reward for Alfieri's murder, poured out to his brother, moved and reconciled to him by the recent fear of his death, all his grievances against the Tuscan Court, against his wife, and against her lover. A letter of Sir Horace Mann makes it clear that Charles Edward persuaded his brother that his ill-usage of his wife (which, however, Mann, with his spies everywhere, had vouched for at the time) was a mere invention, and part of an odious plot by which Alfieri had imposed upon the Grand Duke, the Pope, the society of Florence and Rome, nay, upon Cardinal York himself, in order to obtain their connivance in a shameful intrigue development. The Cardinal returned to Rome in a state of indignation proportionate to his previous saintly indifference to the doings of Alfieri and Mme. d'Albany; he discovered that he had been shutting his eyes to what all the world (by Alfieri's own confession) saw as a very hazardous state of things; and, with the tendency to run into extremes of a foolish and weak-minded creature, he immediately published from all the housetops the dishonour whose existence had never occurred to him before. To the Countess of Albany he intimated that he would not permit her to receive Alfieri under his roof; and of the Pope (the Pope who had so recently patted Alfieri's cheek) he immediately implored an order that Alfieri should quit the Papal States within a fortnight. The order was given; but Alfieri, in whose truthfulness I have complete faith, says that, knowing that the order had been asked for, he forestalled the ignominy of being banished by spontaneously bidding farewell to the Countess of Albany and to Rome.

"This event," says Alfieri, "upset my brains for nearly two years; and upset and retarded also my work in every way." In speaking of Alfieri's youth I have already had occasion to remark that there was in this man's character something abnormal; he was, as I have said, a moral invalid from birth; his very energy and resolution had somewhat of the frenzy and rigidity of a nervous disease, and though he would seem morally stronger than other men when strictly following his self-prescribed rule of excessive intellectual exercise, and when surrounded by a soothing atmosphere of affection and encouragement, his old malady of melancholy and rage (melancholy and rage whom he represents in one of his sonnets as two horrible-faced women seated on either side of him), his old incapacity for work, for interest in anything, his old feverish restlessness of place, returned, as a fever returns with its heat and cold and impotence and delirium, whenever he was shut out of this atmosphere of happiness, whenever he was exposed to any sort of moral hardship. On leaving Rome Alfieri went to Siena, where, years before, when he had come light-hearted and bent only upon literary fame, to learn Tuscan, he had been introduced into a little circle of men and women whom he faithfully loved, and to that Francesco Gori who shared with Tommaso di Caluso the rather trying honour of being his bosom friend. This Gori, "an incomparable man," writes Alfieri, "good, compassionate, and with all his austerity and ruggedness of virtue (*con tanta altezza e ferocia di sensi*) most gentle," appears literally to have nursed Alfieri in this period of moral sickness as one might nurse a sick or badly-bruised child. "Without him," writes Alfieri, "I think I should most likely have gone mad. But he, although he saw in me a would-be hero so disgracefully broken in spirit and inferior to himself" (this passage is characteristic, as showing that Alfieri considered himself, when in a normal condition, far superior to his much-praised Gori), "although he knew better than any the meaning of courage and endurance, did not, therefore, cruelly and inopportunely, oppose his severe and frozen reason to my frenzies, but, on the contrary, diminished my pain by dividing it with me. O rare, O truly heavenly gift, this of being able both to reason and to feel."

Weeping and raving, Alfieri was living once more upon letters received and sent as during his previous separation from Mme. d'Albany; and of all these love-letters, none appear to have come down to us. Carefully preserved by Mme. d'Albany and by her heir Fabre, they fell into the hands of a Mr. Gache of Montpellier, who assumed the grave responsibility of destroying them and of thus suppressing for ever the most important evidence in the law-suit which posterity will for ever be bringing against Alfieri and Mme. d'Albany in favour of Charles Edward, or against Charles Edward in favour of Alfieri and Mme. d'Albany. But some weeks ago, among the pile of the Countess's letters to Sienese friends preserved by Cavaliere Guiseppe Porri at Siena, I had the good fortune to discover what are virtually five love-letters of hers, obviously intended for Alfieri although addressed to his friend Francesco Gori. I confess that an eerie feeling came over me as I unfolded these five closely-written, unsigned and undated little squares of yellow paper, things intended so exclusively for the mere moment of writing and reading, all that long-dead momentary passion of a long-dead man and woman quivering back into reality, filling, as an assembly of ghosts might fill a house, and drive out its living occupants, this present hour which so soon will itself have become, with all its passions and worries, a part of the past, of the indifferent, the passionless. One is frightened on suddenly being admitted to witness, unperceived, as by the opening of a long-locked door, or by some spell said over a crystal globe or a beryl-stone, such passion as this; one feels as if one would almost rather not. These five letters, as I have said, are addressed to a "Dear Signor Francesco, friend of my friend," and who, of course, is Francesco Gori; and are written, which no other letters of Mme. d'Albany's are, not in French, but in tolerably idiomatic though far from correct Italian. Only one of them has any indication of place or date, "Genzano, Mardi"; but this, and the references to Alfieri's approaching journey northward and to Gori's intention of escorting him as far as Genoa, is sufficient to show that they must have been written in the summer of 1783, when Cardinal York, terrified at the liberty which he had allowed to his sister-in-law, had conveyed her safely to some villa in the Alban Hills. The woman who wrote these letters is a strangely different being from the quiet jog-trot, rather cynically philosophical Countess of Albany whom we know from all her other innumerable manuscript letters, from the published answers of Sismondi, of Foscolo and of Mme. de Souza to letters of hers which have disappeared. The hysterical frenzy of Alfieri seems to have entered into this woman; he has worked up this naturally placid but malleable soul, this woman in bad health, deprived of all friends, jealously guarded by enemies, weak and depressed, until she has become another himself, "weeping, raving," like himself, but unable to relieve, perhaps to enjoy, all this frantic grief by running about like the mad Orlando, or talking and weeping by the hour to a compassionate Gori.

> "Dear Signor Francesco," she writes; "how grateful I am to
> you for your compassion. You can't have a notion of our
> unhappiness. My misery is not in the least less than that
> of our friend. There are moments when I feel my heart
> torn to pieces thinking of all that he must suffer. I have
> no consolation except your being with him, and that is
> something. Never let him remain alone. He is worse, and
> I know that he greatly enjoys your society, for you are the

only person who does not bore him and whom he always meets with pleasure. Oh! dear Signor Francesco, in what a sea of miseries are we not! You also, because our miseries are certainly also yours. I no longer live; and if it were not for my friend, for whom I am keeping myself, I would not drag out this miserable life. What do I do in this world? I am a useless creature in it; and why should I suffer when it is of no use to anyone? But my friend—I cannot make up my mind to leave him, and he must live for his own glory; and, as long as he lives, even if I had to walk on my hands, I would suffer and live. Who knows what will happen, it is so long since the man in Florence (Charles Edward) is ill, and still he lives, and it seems to me that he is made of iron in order that we may all die. You will say, in order to console me, that he can't last; but I see things clearly. This illness has not made him younger, but he may live another couple of years. He may at any moment be suffocated by the humours which have risen to his chest. What a cruel thing to expect one's happiness from the death of another! O God! how it degrades one's soul! And yet I cannot refrain from wishing it. What a thing, what a horrible thing is life; and for me it has been a continual suffering, all except the two years that I spent with my friend, and even then I lived in the midst of tears. And you also are probably not happy; with a heart like yours it is not possible that you should be. Whoever is born with any feeling can scarcely enjoy happiness. I recommend our friend to your care, particularly his health. Mine is not so bad; I take care of myself and stay much in bed to kill the time and to rest my nerves, which are very weak. Good-bye, dear Signor Francesco, preserve your friendship for me; I deserve it, since I appreciate you."

Later on she writes again:—

"Dear Signor Francesco, friend of ours. I do all I can to take courage. I study as much as I can. Music alone distracts my thoughts, or rather deadens them, and I play the harp many hours a day, and I do so also because I know that my friend wishes me to get to play it well. I work at it as hard as I can.

I live only for him; without him life would be odious to me, and I could not endure it. I do nothing in this world; I am useless in it; and where is the use of suffering for nothing? But there is my friend, and I must remain on this earth. I do not doubt of him; I know how much he loves me. But in moments of suffering I have fears lest he should find someone who would give him less pain than myself, with whom he might live cheerful and happy. I ought to wish it, but I have not got the strength to do so. But I believe so fully in him that I am satisfied as soon as he tells me that such a thing cannot happen. I love him more than myself; it is a union of feeling which we only can understand. I find in him all that I can desire; he is everything for me; and yet I must suffer separation from him. Certainly if I could come to a violent decision I should be the happiest woman in the world; I should never think of the past; I should live in him and for him; for I care for nothing in this world. Comfort, luxury, position, all is vanity for me; peace by his side would suffice for me. And yet I am condemned to languish far from him. What a horrible life!"

Again she writes to Gori:—

"Dear friend, I am so very, very grateful for the interest you take in my unhappy situation, which is really terrible. Time serves only to aggravate it, and certainly it will bring no alleviation to my misery until I shall meet our friend. There is no peace, no tranquillity for me. I would give whatever of life may remain to me in order to live for one day with him, and I should be satisfied. My feelings for him are unchangeable, and I am sure that his for me are the same. When shall I see the end of my woes? Who knows whether I shall ever see it? That man (Charles Edward) does not seem inclined to depart. . . I suffer a little from my nerves. . . but those are the least of my sufferings. It is the heart which suffers. I have moments of despair when I could throw myself out of the window were it not for the thought that I must live for my friend's sake; that my life is his. I feel a disgust for life which is so reasoned out that I say to myself sometimes,

'Why do I live? What good do I do?' and then I continue
to suffer patiently, remembering my friend. Forgive me for
unbosoming myself with you, who alone can understand
me; you alone, except my friend, understand what I suffer.
Do you know, you ought to come and see me this winter,
you would give me such a pleasure. Good-bye, dear Signor
Francesco; preserve your friendship for me."

Thus she runs on, repeating and re-repeating the same ideas, the
same words, her love for Alfieri, her desperate situation, her hatred of
life, her uselessness, her desire to play the harp well for Alfieri's sake,
her hopes that Charles Edward may die; disconnected phrases, run into
each other without so much as a comma or a full stop (since I have had
to punctuate my translation, at least partially, to make it intelligible);
the excited, unconsecutive, unceasing, discursive, reiterating gabble of
hysteria, eager, vague, impotent, thoughts suddenly vanishing and as
suddenly coming to a dead stop; everything rattled off as if between
two sobs or two convulsions. Did Alfieri enjoy receiving letters such
as these? Doubtless: they were echoes of his own ravings; fuel for his
own passion and vanity. It did not strike him, for all the Greek and
Roman heroes and heroines whom he had made to speak with stoical,
unflinching curtness, that there could be anything to move shame,
and compassion sickened by shame, in the fact that this should be
the expression of that high and pure love imitated from Dante and
Petrarch. What could he do? Give up Louise d'Albany, forget her; and
bid her, who lived only in him, whom a few years must free, forget him
at the price of breaking her heart? Certainly not. But he, the man, the
man free to move about, to work, with friends and occupations, should
surely have tried to teach resignation and patience to this poor lonely,
sick, hysterical woman, pointing out to her that if only they would
wait, and wait courageously, the moment of liberation and happiness
must come. Surely more difficult and humiliating for this lover to bear
than the sight of his lady degraded by the foul words and deeds of the
drunken Pretender, ought to have been the reading of such letters as
these; the sight of this once calm and dignified woman, of this Beatrice
or Laura, in her disconnected hysterical ravings. And for myself, the
thought of all that the Countess of Albany endured at the hands of
Charles Edward awakens less pity, though pity mixed with indignation
at the fate which humiliated her so deeply, and with shame for that

deep humiliation, than that sudden cry with which she stops in the midst of the light-headed gabble about her miseries, and seems to start back ashamed as at the sight of her passion and tear-defiled face in a mirror: "What a cruel thing to expect one's happiness from the death of another! O God! how it degrades one's soul!"

XII

COLMAR

O n the 17th August 1784, at eight in the morning, at the inn of the *Two Keys*, Colmar, I met her, and remained speechless from excess of joy." So runs an annotation of Alfieri on the margin of one of his lyrics.

The hour of liberty and happiness had come for Alfieri and Mme. d'Albany; sooner by far than they expected, and sooner, we may think, than they deserved. Liberty and happiness, however, not in the face of the law. Charles Edward was still alive; but, pressed by King Gustavus III of Sweden, whom he contrived to wheedle out of some most unnecessary money, he had consented to a legal separation from his fugitive wife; as a result of which the Countess of Albany, renouncing all money supplies from the Stuarts, and subsisting entirely upon a share of the two pensions, French and Papal, granted to her husband, was permitted to spend a portion of the year wheresoever she pleased, provided she returned for awhile to show herself in the Papal States. On hearing the unexpected news, Alfieri, who was crossing the Apennines of Modena with fourteen horses that he had been to buy in England, was seized with a violent temptation to send his caravan along the main road, and gallop by cross-paths to meet the Countess, who was crossing the Apennines of Bologna on her way from Rome to the baths of Baden in Switzerland. The thought of her honour and safety restrained him, and he pushed on moodily to Siena. But, as on a previous occasion, his stern resolution not to seek his lady soon gave way; and two months later followed that meeting at the *Two Keys* at Colmar on the Rhine.

For the first time in those seven long years of platonic passion, Alfieri and Mme. d'Albany found themselves settled beneath the same roof. To the mind of this Italian man, and this half-French, half-German woman of the eighteenth century, for whom marriage was one of the sacraments of a religion in which they wholly disbelieved, and one of the institutions of a society which alleviated it with universal adultery; to Alfieri and Mme. d'Albany the legal separation from Charles Edward Stuart was equivalent to a divorce. The Pretender could no longer prescribe any line of conduct to his wife; she was free to live where and with whom she chose; and if she were not free to marry, the idea, the wish for marriage, probably never crossed the brains of these two platonic lovers of seven years' standing. Marriage was a social contract between people who wished to obtain each other's money and titles and lands—who wished to have heirs. Alfieri, who had made over all his property to his sister, and the Countess, who lived on a pension, had no money or titles or lands to throw together; and they certainly neither of them, the man living entirely for his work, the woman living entirely for the man, had the smallest desire to have children, heirs to nothing at all. What injury could their living together now do to Charles Edward, who had relinquished all his husband's rights? None, evidently. On the other hand, what harm could their living together do to their own honour or happiness, now that they had had seven years' experience that only death could extinguish their affection? None, again evidently. And as to harm to the institutions of society, what were those institutions, and what was their value, that they should be respected? Such, could we have questioned them, would have been the answers of Alfieri and the Countess. That they were setting an example to others less pure in mind, less exceptional in position; that they were making it more difficult for marriage to be reorganised on a more rational plan, by showing men and women a something that might do instead of rationally organised marriage; that they were, in short, preventing the law from being rectified, by taking the law into their own hands: such thoughts could not enter into the mind of continentals of the eighteenth century, people for whom the great Revolution, Romanticism, and the new views of society which grew out of both, were still in the future. That a punishment should await them, that as time went on and youthful passion diminished, their lives should be barren and silent and cold for want of all those things: children, legal bonds, social recognition, by which their union should fall short of a real marriage; this they could never anticipate.

For the moment, united in the "excessively clean and comfortable" little château, rented by Madame d'Albany at a short distance from Colmar; riding and driving about in the lovely Rhine country; the Countess deep in her reading again, Alfieri deep once more in his writings; together, above all, after so many months of separation: they seemed perfectly happy. So happy that it seemed as if a misfortune must come to restore the natural balance of things; and the misfortune came, in the sudden news of the death of poor Francesco Gori. A sense as of guiltiness at having half forgotten that thoughtful and gentle friend in the first flush of their happiness, seems to have come over them.

"O God," wrote Alfieri to Gori's friend Bianchi at Siena, "I don't know what I shall do. I always see him and speak to him, and every smallest word and thought and gesture of his returns to my mind, and stabs my heart. I do not feel very sorry for him: he cared little for life for its own sake, and the life which he was forced to lead was too far below his great soul, and the goodness and tenderness of his heart, and the nobility of his noble scornfulness. The person dearest to me of any, and immediately next to whom I loved Checco (Gori) most, knew and appreciated him and is not to be consoled for such a loss. I told him already last July, so many, many times, that he was not well, that he was growing visibly thinner day by day. Oh! I ought never to have left him in this state."

A letter, this one on Gori's death, which may induce us to forgive the letters of Alfieri of which we have seen a reflection in those of Mme. d'Albany: the passionate grief for the lost friend making us feel that there is something noble in the possibility of even the morbid grief at the lost mistress. More touching still, bringing home what each of us, alas! must have felt in those long, dull griefs for one who is not our kith and kin, whom the thoughts of our nearest and dearest, of our work, of all those things which the world recognises as ours in a sense in which the poor beloved dead was not, does not permit us to mourn in such a way as to satisfy our heart, and the longing for whom, half suppressed, comes but the more pertinaciously to haunt us, to make the present and future, all where he or she is not, a blank; more touching than any letter in which Alfieri gives free vent to his grief for poor Gori, is that note which he wrote upon the manuscript of his poem on Duke Alexander's murder, after the annotation saying that this work was resumed at Siena, the 17th July 1784—"O God! and the friend of my heart was still living then"; the words which a man speaks, or writes only for himself, feeling that no one, not those even who are the very flesh and blood of his heart, can, since they are not himself, feel that terrible pang at suddenly seeing the past so close within his reach, so hopelessly beyond his grasp.

The death of Gori seemed the only circumstance which diminished the happiness of Alfieri and Mme. d'Albany; nay, it is not heartless, surely, to say that, cruel as was that wound, there was doubtless a quite special sad sweetness in each trying to heal it in the other, in the redoubled love due to this fellow-feeling in affliction, the new energy of affection which comes to the survivors whenever Death calls out the warning, "Love each other while I still let you." But they had still to pay, and pay in many instalments, the price of happiness snatched before its legitimate time.

Supposed to be living apart from Alfieri, the Countess could not, therefore, take him back with her to Italy, where, according to the stipulations of the act of separation, she was bound to spend the greater part of every year. Hence the stay at Colmar in 1784, and those in the succeeding years, were merely so many interludes of happiness in the dreary life of separation; happiness which, as Alfieri says in one of his sonnets, was constantly embittered by the thought that every day and every hour was bringing them nearer to a cruel parting. The day came: Alfieri had to take leave of Mme. d'Albany; and, as he expresses it, had to return to much worse gloom than before, being separated from his lady without having the consolation of seeing Gori once more. Mechanically he returned to Siena, to Siena which it was impossible to conceive without his friend Checco; but when he realised the empty house, the empty town, he found the place he had so loved insupportable, and went to spend his long solitary winter writing, reading, translating, breaking in horses, leading a slave's life to pass the weary time, at Pisa. In April 1785 Mme. d'Albany obtained permission to quit Bologna, where she had spent the winter, and to go to her sisters in France. In September she and her lover met once more in the beloved country-house on the Rhine. But again, in December, came another separation; Mme. d'Albany went to Paris, and Alfieri remained behind at Colmar.

"Shall we then be again separated," he writes in a sonnet, "by cruel and lying opinion, which blames us for errors which the whole world commits every day? Unhappy that I am! The more I love thee with true and loyal love, the more must I ever refuse myself that for which I am always longing: thy sweet sight, beyond which I ask for nothing. But the vulgar cannot understand this, and knows us but little, and does not see that thy pure heart is the seat of virtue."

Strange words, and which, coming from a man cynical and truthful as Alfieri, may make us pause and refuse to affirm that this strange love, platonic for seven long years, ceased to be a mere passionate friendship even when it resorted to the secrecy and deceptions of a mere common intrigue; even when it openly braved, in the semblance of marriage, the opinion of the world at large. During those many months of solitude in the villa at Colmar, with no other company than that of his Sienese servant or secretary and of the horses, whose news he carefully sent, in letters and sonnets, to the Countess, Alfieri appears for the first time to have got into a habit of excessive overwork, and to have had the first serious attack of the gout; overwork and gout, the two things which were to kill him. A six months' stay in Paris, where society, the business of printing his works, and the great distance of his lodgings from the house of Mme. d'Albany, diminished his intellectual work, kept him up for the moment. But in the following summer of the year 1787, shortly after he had returned to Colmar with the Countess, and had welcomed as a guest Tommaso di Caluso, his greatest friend since Gori's death, he suddenly broke down under a terrific attack of dysentery. For many days, reduced to a skeleton, ice cold even under burning applications, and just sufficiently alive to feel in his intensely proud and masculine nature the cruel degradation of an illness which made him an object of loathing to himself, Alfieri remained at death's door, devotedly tended by his beloved and by his friend.

"It grieved me dreadfully to think that I should die, leaving my lady, and my friend, and that fame scarcely rough hewn for which I had worked and frenzied myself so terribly for more than ten years," writes Alfieri; "for I felt very keenly that of all the writings which I should leave behind me, not one was completed and finished as it should have been had time been given me to complete and to perfect according to my ideas. On the other hand, it was a great consolation to know that, if I must die, I should die a free man, and between the two best beloved persons that I had, and whose love and esteem I believed myself to possess and to deserve."

Alfieri recovered. But with that illness ends, I think, the period of his youth, and of his genius, that is to say, of that high-wrought and passionate austerity and independence of character which was to him what artistic endowment is to other writers; and with that illness begins a premature old age, mental and moral, decrepitude gradually showing itself in a kind of ossification of the whole personality; the decrepitude which corresponds, on the other side of a brief manhood of comparative strength and health, to the morally inert and sickly years of Alfieri's strange youth.

XIII

RUE DE BOURGOYNE

Alfieri's mother, an old lady of extreme simplicity of mind and gentleness of spirit, was still living at Asti, cheerfully depriving herself of every luxury in order to devote her fortune, as she devoted her thoughts and her strength, to the services of the poor and of the sick. Alfieri, who had left her as a boy, and scarcely seen her except for a few hours at rare intervals, looked up to her less with the affection of a son than with the satisfaction of an artist who sees in the woman of whom he is born the peculiar type of features or character which he prizes most in womankind; if he, for all his conscious weaknesses, was more like his own heroes than any man of his acquaintance, if Mme. d'Albany might be judiciously got up as the Laura of his affections, the old Countess Alfieri was even more unmistakably the mother who suited his ideas, the living model of his mother of Virginia, or his mother of Myrrha. To the Countess Alfieri he had, already in 1784, introduced the Countess of Albany, whom she invited to stay with her on her passage through Asti as she returned from Colmar into Italy. Mme. d'Albany found an excuse for not accepting in the bad state of the roads, which rendered another route than that of Asti preferable. Frank and indifferent to the world's opinion as was Mme. d'Albany, her originally cut and dry intellectual temper hardened by many years' misery, one can conceive that she should shrink from accepting the hospitality of Alfieri's mother. Alfieri had doubtless shown her his mother's letters, and from these letters, as reflected in his answers, it is clear that the Countess of Albany, returning from that first stay with her lover at Colmar, would have felt that she was tacitly deceiving the noble old lady under whose roof she was staying. For the Countess Alfieri, noble, and Italian, and woman of the eighteenth century though she was, seems to have been one of those persons into whose mind, high removed above all worldly concerns, no experience of vice, of weakness, nay, of mere equivocal situations, can enter. Whatever she may have seen or heard in her youth of the habits of women of her century and station, of the virtual divorce which, after a few years, reigned in aristocratic houses, of authorised lovers and socially accepted infidelity, seems to have passed out of her memory and left her mind as innocent as it may have been during her convent school-days. She had taken great interest in this poor young woman, maltreated by a drunken husband, and finally saved from his clutches by the benevolence of the Grand Duke of Tuscany and of a prince of the church, about whom her son had written to her. That her son experienced more than her own pity for so worthy an object, that he was at all compromised in the fate of this virtuous, unhappy lady, never entered her mind. So little could she understand the muddy things of this world, that in 1789, when Alfieri was publicly living with Mme. d'Albany at Colmar, the Countess Alfieri sent him, through his friend Caluso, the suggestion of a match which she had greatly at heart, between him and a young lady of Asti, "fifteen or sixteen years old, without any faults, such as he would certainly like, cultivated, docile, and clever." It is one of the things which grate upon one most in Alfieri's character, and which show that however much he might be cast and have chiselled himself in antique heroic form he was yet made of the same stuff as his contemporaries, to find that he and his friend Caluso merely amused themselves immensely at this proposal of marriage, and concocted a dutiful letter to the old Countess explaining that matrimony was not at present in his plans. What would Madame Alfieri have thought had she known the truth! It is very sad to think how, in some cases, the very noblest and purest, just because they are so completely noble and pure and above all the base necessities of the world of passion, must be unable to see, in the doings of others less fortunate than themselves, those very elements of nobility and purity which redeem the baser circumstances of their lives. That Mme. d'Albany had loved a man not her husband, had fled from her husband and united her life to that of her lover, would be a horror visible to the old Countess' eyes; the platonic purity, the fidelity, the loyalty of this long and illegitimate love, would have escaped her. No art is so cruelly contemptuous of whatever of beauty and sweetness imperfect reality may contain, as the art which is able to attain an ideal perfection; and thus it is also in matters of appreciation of man by man and woman by woman. The Countess of Albany was apparently more frank than Alfieri, because frank rather from temperament than from pre-occupation about a given ideal of conduct. That the mother of Alfieri should understand so little seems to have worried her; and when the unsuspecting old lady asked her sympathisingly for news of Charles Edward, she wrote back as follows: "As to my husband, he is better; but I must confess to you, Madame, that I cannot take so lively an interest in him as you suppose, for he made me, during nine years, the most wretched woman that ever lived. If I do not hate him it is a result of Christian charity, and because we are desired to pardon. He drags out a miserable life, abandoned by all the world, without relatives or friends, given over to his servants; but he has willed it thus, since he has never been able to live with anyone. Forgive me, Madame, for having entered into such details with you; but the friendship which you have shown towards me obliges me to speak sincerely." Mme. d'Albany, writing some time before to condole about the death of Alfieri's half-brother, had tried to insinuate to the old Countess what her son was for her, and what position she herself might one day assume in the Alfieri family: "I hope that if circumstances change, you will not see a family die out to which you are so attached, and that you will receive the greatest consolation from M. le Comte Alfieri." Words which could only mean that when the Pretender died Mme. Alfieri might hope for a daughter-in-law in the writer, and for grand-children through her. But Madame Alfieri did not understand; imagining, perhaps, that Mme. d'Albany was alluding to some project of marriage of her friend M. le Comte Alfieri; and the letter in which the ill-treated wife's aversion to her husband was first openly revealed appears to have acted as a thunder-clap, and to have, at least momentarily, put an end to all correspondence.

The Countess of Albany was mistaken in supposing that Charles Edward would die in the arms of mere servants. The very year after her own separation from Alfieri, the Pretender had called to Florence the natural daughter born to him by Miss Walkenshaw, and whom he had left, apparently forgotten for twenty-five years, in the convent at Meaux, where her mother had taken refuge from his brutalities, even as Louise d'Albany had taken refuge from them in the convent of the Bianchette. Partly from a paternal feeling born of the unexpected solitude in which his wife's flight had left him; partly, doubtless, from a desire to spite the Countess; he had solemnly, as King of England, legitimated this daughter, and created her Duchess of Albany: he had made incredible efforts, abandoning drink, going into the world and keeping open house, to attach this young woman to him, and to treat her as well as he had treated his wife ill.

Charlotte of Albany, a strong, lively, good-humoured, big creature, devoted to gaiety, effectually reformed her father in his last years, and turned him, from the brute he had been, to a tolerably well-behaved old man. But we must not therefore conclude that Charlotte was a better woman, or a woman more desirous of doing her duty, than Louise d'Albany. Between the two there was an abyss: Charlotte had been sent for by a man weary of solitude, smarting under the frightful punishment brought upon his pride by the flight of his wife; ready to do anything in order not to be alone and despised by the world; a man broken by illness and age, weak, hysterical, incapable almost of his former excesses; and Charlotte was a woman of thirty, she was a daughter, she was free to go where she would to marry, and her father could buy her presence only at the price of submission to her tastes and to her desires. How different had it not been with Louise of Stolberg: united to this man twelve years before, a mere child of nineteen, given over to him as his wife, his chattel, his property, to torment and lock up as he might torment and lock up his dog or his horse; losing all influence over him with every day which made her less of a novelty and diminished the chance of an heir; and sickened and alarmed more and more by the obstinate jealousy and drunkenness and brutality of a man still in the vigour of his odious passions. Still, the fact remains that while Louise d'Albany was secretly or openly making light of all social institutions, and living as the mistress, almost the wife, of Alfieri; this insignificant Charlotte, this bastard of a Miss Walkenshaw, this woman who had probably never had an enthusiasm, or an ideal, or a thought, had succeeded in reclaiming whatever there remained of human in the degraded Charles Edward; had succeeded in doing the world the service of laying out at least with decency and decorum this living corpse which had once contained the soul of a hero, so that posterity might look upon it without too much contempt and loathing, nay, almost, seeing it so quiet and seemingly peaceful, with compassion and reverence.

And when, at the beginning of February 1788, the Countess of Albany, in the full enjoyment of her love for Alfieri, and of the pleasures of the most brilliant Parisian society, received the news that on the last day of January Charles Edward had passed away peacefully in the arms of the Duchess Charlotte; and that the drink-soiled broken body, from which she must so often have recoiled in disgust and terror, had been laid out, with the sad mock royalty of a gilt wooden sceptre and pinchbeck crown, in state in the cathedral of Frascati; when, I say, the news reached Paris, this woman, so confident of having been in the right, and who had written so frankly that if she did not hate her husband it was from mere Christian charity and the duty of forgiveness, felt herself smitten by an unexpected grief.

Alfieri, who witnessed it with astonishment, and to whose cut-and-dry nature it must have seemed highly mysterious, was, nevertheless, in a way overawed by this sudden emotion at the death of the man who had made both lovers so miserable. His appreciation, difficult to so narrow a temper, of all that may move our sympathy in that, to him, unintelligible grief, is, I think, one of the facts in his life which brings this strange, artificial, heroic, admirable, yet repulsive character, most within reach of our affection; as that same grief, so unexpected by herself, at what was after all her final deliverance, is, together with the letter to Alfieri's mother, telling of her hatred to Charles Edward, and that exclamation in the hysterical love-letter at Siena—"O God! how this degrades the soul!"—one of the things which persuade us that this woman, whom we shall see inconsistent, worldly, and cynical, did really possess at bottom what her lover called "a most upright and sincere and incomparable soul."

"For the present," wrote Alfieri to his Sienese friends on the occasion of Charles Edward's death, "nothing will be altered in our mode of life." In other words, the Countess of Albany and her lover, established publicly beneath the same roof in Paris, did not intend getting married. Whatever hopes may have filled Mme. d'Albany's heart when, years before, she had hinted to Alfieri's mother that when certain circumstances changed, the Alfieri family should be saved from extinction; whatever ideas Alfieri had had in his mind when he prayed in a sonnet for the happy day when he might call his love holy; whatever intention of repairing the injury done to social institutions, may at one time have mingled with the lovers' remorse and the lovers' temptations,—had now been completely forgotten. We have seen how, more than once, love, however self-restrained, had induced Alfieri to put aside all his Republican sternness and truthfulness, and to cringe before people whom he thoroughly despised; we cannot easily forget that ignominious stroking of the Brutus poet's cheek by Pope Pius VI. We shall now see how this peculiar sort of Roman and stoical virtue, cultivated by Alfieri in himself and in his beloved as the one admirable thing in the world, a strange exotic in this eighteenth-century baseness, had nevertheless withered in several of its branches, beaten by the wind of illegitimate passion, and dried up by the callousness of an immoral state of society: an exotic, or rather a precocious moral variety, come before its season, and bleached and warped like a winter flower.

Alfieri and the Countess did not get married, simply, I think, because they did not care to get married; because marriage would entail reorganisation of a mode of life which had somehow organised itself; because it would give a common-place prose solution to what appeared a romantic and exceptional story; and finally because it might necessitate certain losses in the way of money, of comfort, and of rank.

One sees throughout all his autobiography and letters that Alfieri drew a sharp distinction between love and marriage; that he conceived marriage as the act of a man who sets up shop, so to say, in his native place, goes in for having children, for being master in his own house, administering and increasing his estates, and generally devoting himself to the advancement of his family. As such Alfieri, who was essentially a routinist, respected and approved of marriage; and anything different would have struck his martinet, rule and compass, mind, as ridiculous and contemptible. In giving up his fortune to his sister, Alfieri had deliberately cut himself off from the possibility of such a marriage; moreover, putting aside the financial question, his notion of the liberty of a writer, who must be able to speak freely against any government, was incompatible with his notion of a father of a family, settled in dignity in his ancestral palace; and finally, I feel perfectly persuaded that in the mind of Alfieri, which saw things only in sharpest black and white contrasts, there existed a still more complete incompatibility between a woman like the Countess of Albany, and a wife such as he conceived a wife: to marry Mme. d'Albany would be to degrade a poetical ideal into vulgar domesticity, and at the same time to frightfully depart from the normal type of matrimony, which required that the man be absolute master, and not afflicted with any sort of sentimental respect for his better half.

According to Alfieri, there were two possibilities for the ideal man: a handsome and highly respectable marriage with a girl twenty years his junior, fresh from the convent, provided with the right number of heraldic quarterings, acres, diamonds, and domestic virtues, and who would bear him, in deep awe for his unapproachable superiority, five or six robust children; and a romantic connexion with a married woman or a widow, a woman all passion and intellect and aspiration, with whom he should go through a course of mutual soul improvement, who should be the sharer of all his higher life, and whom he would diligently deck out as a Beatrice or a Laura in the eyes of society.

The Countess of Albany did not fit into the first ideal; nor, for the matter of that, did Alfieri, poor, expatriated, mad for independence, engrossed in literature, fit into it himself; and both, as it happened, fitted in perfectly to the second ideal possibility. To get married with a view to turning into domestic beings, would be a failure, a trouble, an interruption, a desecration, and a bore; to get married merely to go on as they were at present, would, in the eyes of Alfieri, have been a profanation of the poetry of their situation, a perfectly unnecessary piece of humbug.

Such were, doubtless, Alfieri's views of the case. Mme. d'Albany, on the other hand, had evidently no vocation as a housewife or a mother; marriage was full of disagreeable associations to her: a husband might beat one, and a lover might not. She, probably, also, guessed instinctively that to Alfieri a Laura must always be a mere mistress, and a wife must always be a mere Griselda; she knew his cut-and-dry views, his frightful power of carrying theory into practice; she may have guessed that the most respectful of lovers would in his case make the most tyrannical of husbands. But while Alfieri doubtless brought Mme. d'Albany to share his abstract reasons, Mme. d'Albany probably brought home to him her own more practical ones. Alfieri, we must remember, had been a man of excessive social vanity; and much as he despised mankind, he certainly still liked to enjoy its admiring consideration. Mme. d'Albany, on the other hand, had been brought up in the full worldliness of a canoness of Ste. Wandru, and had grown accustomed to a certain amount of state and of luxury; and these worldly tendencies, thrown into the background by the passion, the poetry which sprang up with the irresistible force of a pressed down spring during her married misery, had returned to her as years went on, and as passion cooled and poetry diminished. Now marriage would probably involve a great risk of a diminution of income, since the Pope and the Court of France might easily refuse to support Charles Edward's widow once she had ceased to be a Stuart; and it must inevitably mean an end to a quasi-regal mode of life to which the widow of the Pretender could lay claim, but the wife of a Piedmontese noble could not. It is one of the various meannesses, committed quite unconsciously by Mme. d'Albany, and apparently not censured by the people of the eighteenth century, that, so far from being anxious to shake off all vestiges of her hateful married life, the Countess of Albany, on the contrary, seemed determined to enjoy, so to speak, her money's worth; to get whatever advantages had been bought at the price of her marriage with Charles Edward. Mme. d'Albany enjoyed being the widow of a kind of sovereign. Rather easy-going and familiar by nature, she nevertheless assumed towards strangers a certain queenly haughtiness which frequently gave offence; and Sir Nathaniel Wraxall, who was introduced at her house in 1788, found, to his surprise, that all the plate belonging to Mme. d'Albany was engraved with the royal arms of England; that guests were conducted through an ante-room in which stood a royal throne also emblazoned with the arms of England; nay, that the servants had orders to address the lady of the house by the title of a queen: a state of things whose institution by a woman who affected nobility of sentiment and who made no secret of her hatred of Charles Edward, whose toleration by a man who scorned the world and abhorred royalty, is one of those strange anomalies which teach us the enormous advance in self-respect and self-consistency due to social and democratic progress, an improvement which separates in feeling even the most mediocre and worldly men and women of today from the most high-minded and eccentric men and women of a century ago. To marry Alfieri would mean, for the Countess of Albany, to risk part of her fortune and to relinquish her royal state, as well as to sink into a mere humdrum housewife. Hence, in both parties concerned, a variety of reasons, contemptible in our eyes, excellent in their own, against legitimating their connection. And, on the other hand, no corresponding inducement. Why should they get married? The Countess, going in state every Sunday to a convent where she was received with royal honours, Alfieri writing to his mother that although he was not regular at confession, he was yet provided with a most austere and worthy spiritual director in case of need, neither of them had the smallest belief in Christianity nor in its sacraments. To please whom should they marry, pray? To please religion? Why, they had none. To please society? Why, society, in this Paris of the year 1788, at least such aristocratic society as they cared to see, consisted entirely either of devoted couples of high-minded lovers each with a husband or wife somewhere in the background, or of even more interesting triangular arrangements of high-minded and devoted wife, husband, and lover, all living together on charming terms, and provided, in case of disagreement, each with a *lettre de cachet* which should lock the other up in the Bastille. A Queen of England by right divine, keeping open house in company with a ferociously republican Piedmontese poet, was indeed a new and perhaps a questionable case; but the pre-revolutionary society of Paris was too philosophical to be surprised at anything; and, after very little hesitation, resorted to the charming Albany-Alfieri hotel in the Rue de Bourgoyne. Now, if the well-born and amusing people in Paris did not insist upon Alfieri and the Countess getting married, why should they go out of their way to do so? We good people of the nineteenth century should have liked them the better; but then, you see, it was the peculiarity of the men and women of the eighteenth century to be quite unable to conceive that the men and women of the nineteenth century would be in the least different from themselves.

XIV

Before the Storm

The well-born and amusing people of the end of the eighteenth and beginning of the nineteenth century did not stickle at the question of the marriage. They flocked to the hotel of the Rue de Bourgoyne, attracted by the peculiar cosmopolitan charm, the very undeniable talent for society, the extraordinary intellectual superiority of Mme. d'Albany; attracted, also, by a certain easy-going and half-motherly kindliness which seems, to all those who wanted sympathy, to have been quite irresistible. It was the moment of the great fermentation, when even trifling things and trifling people seemed to boil and seethe with importance; when cold-hearted people were suddenly full of tenderness and chivalry, selfish people full of generosity, prosaic people full of poetry, and mediocre people full of genius: the brief carnival-week of the old world, when men and women masqueraded in all manner of outlandish and antiquated thoughts and feelings, and enjoyed the excitement of dressing-up so much that they actually believed themselves for the moment to be what they pretended: it was the brief moment, grotesque and pathetic, when the doomed classes of society, who were fatally going to be exterminated for their long selfishness and indifference, enthusiastically caught up pick-axe and shovel and tore down the bricks of the edifice which was destined to fall and to crush them all beneath its ruins.

All these men and women, their deep in-born corruption momentarily transfigured by this enthusiasm for liberty, for equality, for sentiment, for austerity, which mingled oddly with their childish pleasure in all new things, in mesmerism, in America, in electricity, in Montgolfier balloons, with their habitual pleasure in all their big and small futile and wicked pleasures of worldliness;—all these men and women, these *morituri* delighted at the preparations, the scaffoldings, red clothes, black crape, torches and drums and bugles, for their own execution, all assembled at that hotel of the Rue de Bourgoyne.

A brilliant crowd of ministers and diplomatists, and artists and pamphleteers, and wits and beautiful women; perishable and perished things, out of which we must select one or two, either as types of that which has perished, or as types of the imperishable; and the perished, the amiable and beautiful women, the amusing and brilliantly-improvising orators and philosophers of the half-hour, are often that which, could we have chosen, we should have preserved. Most notable among the women, the young daughter of Necker, the wife of the Swedish ambassador, Mme. la Baronne de Staël Holstein: a rather mannish superb sort of creature, with shoulders and arms compensating for thick swarthy features; eyes like volcanoes; the laugh of the most kind-hearted of children; the stride, the attitude, with her hands for ever behind the back, of an unceremonious man; a young woman already accounted a genius, and felt to be a moral force. Next to her a snub, drab-coloured Livonian, with northern eyes telling of future mysticism, that Mme. de Krüdener, as yet noted only for the droll contrast of her enthusiasm for St. Pierre and the simplicity of nature with her quarterly bills of twenty thousand francs from Mdlle. Bertin, the Queen's milliner; but later to be famous for her literary and religious vagaries, her influence on Mme. de Staël, her strange influence on Alexander of Russia. Near her, doubtless, that fascinating Suard, in the convent of whose sister Mme. de Krüdener was wont to spend a month in religious exercises, thanking God, at the foot of the altar, for giving her a sister like Mdlle. Suard, and a lover like Suard himself. As yet but little noticed, except as the pet friend, the "younger sister" of Mme. d'Albany, a Mme. de Flahault, later married to the Portuguese Souza; a simple-natured little woman, adoring her children and the roses in her garden, and who, if I may judge by the letters which, many, many years later, she addressed to Mme. d'Albany, would be the woman of all those one would rather resuscitate for a friend, leaving Mmes. de Staël and de Krüdener quiet in their coffins. Further on, the delicate and charming Pauline de Beaumont, who was to be the Egeria of Joubert and the tenderly-beloved friend of Châteaubriand; and a host of women notable in those days for wit or heart or looks, wherewith to make a new Ballade of Dead Ladies, much sadder than the one of Villon: "But where are the snows of yester-year?"

Round about these ladies an even greater number of men of what were, or passed for, eminent qualities; political for the most part, or busied with the new science of economy, like the Trudaines; and most notable among them, as the typical victim of genius of the Reign of Terror, poor André Chénier, his exquisite imitations of Theocritus still waiting to be sorted and annotated in prison; and the typical blood-maniac of genius, the painter David, who was to startle Mme. d'Albany's guests, soon after the 10th August, by wishing that the Fishwives had stuck Marie Antoinette's head without more ado upon a pike. Imagine all these people assembled in order to hear M. de Beaumarchais, in the full glory of his millions and his wonderful garden, give a first reading of his *Mère Coupable*, after inviting them to prepare themselves to weep (which was easy in those days of soft hearts) "*à plein canal.*" Or else listening to the cold and solemn M. de Condorcet, prophesying the time when science shall have abolished suffering and shall abolish death; little dreaming of those days of wandering without food, of those nights in the quarries of Montrouge, of that little bottle of poison, the only thing that science could give to abolish his suffering.

To all these great and illustrious people the Countess of Albany—I had almost said the Queen of England—introduced her "incomparable friend" (style then in vogue) Count Vittorio Alfieri; and all of them doubtless took a great interest in him as her lover, and a little interest in him as *the* great poet of Italy; not certainly without wondering—amiable people as they were, and persuaded that France and Paris alone existed—that Mme. d'Albany should find anything to love in this particularly rude and disagreeable man, and that a country like Italy should have the impudence to set up a poet of its own. The Countess of Albany, made to be a leader of intellectual society, was happy; but Alfieri was not. Ever since his childhood, when a French dancing-master had vainly tried to unstiffen his rigid person, he had mortally hated the French nation; ever since his first boyish travels he had loathed Paris as the sewer, the *cloaca maxima* (the expression is his own) of the world; his whole life had been a struggle with the French manners, the French language, which had permeated Piedmont; one of the chief merits of the new drama he had conceived was (in his own eyes) to sweep Corneille, Racine, and particularly Voltaire, his arch-aversion Voltaire, off the stage.

Alfieri, with his faults and his virtues, was specially constructed, if I may use the expression, to ignore all the good points, and to feel with hysterical sensitiveness all the bad ones, of the French nation; and more especially of the French nation of the pre-revolutionary and revolutionary era. Alfieri's reality and Alfieri's ideal were austerity, inflexibility, pride and contemptuousness of character, coldness, roughness, decision of manner, curtness, reticence, and absolute truthfulness of speech; above all, no consideration for other folks' likings and dislikings, no mercy for their foibles. His ideal, even more so than the ideal of other idealising minds, was the mere outcome of himself; it contained his faults as well as his virtues. Now all that fell short of, or went beyond, his ideal—that is to say, himself—was abomination in Alfieri's eyes. Consequently France and the French, all the nobility, the wit, the sentiment, the warm-heartedness, the enthusiasm, the wide-mindedness, the childishness, the frivolity, the instability, the disrespectfulness, the sentimentality, the high falutinism, the superficiality, the looseness of principle, everything that made up the greatness and littleness of the France of the end of last century, everything which will make up the greatness and littleness of France, the glories and weaknesses which the world must love, to the end of time; all these things were abhorrent to Alfieri; and Alfieri, when once he disliked a person or a thing, justly or unjustly, could only increase but never diminish his dislike. Let us look at this matter, which is instructive to all persons whose nobility of character runs to injustice, a little closer; it will help us to understand the *Misogallo*, the extraordinary apostasy which, quite unconsciously, Alfieri was later to commit towards the principle of freedom. Alfieri, intensely Italian, if mediæval and peasant Italy may give us the Italian type, in a certain silent or rather inarticulate violence of temper—violence which roars and yells and stabs and strangles, but which never talks, and much less argues—could not endure the particular sort of excitement which surrounded him in France; excitement mainly cerebral, heroism or villainy resulting, but only as the outcome of argument and definition of principle and of that mixture of logic and rhetoric called by the French *des mots*. Alfieri was not a reasoning mind, he was not an eloquent man; above all, he was not a witty man; his satirical efforts are so many blows upon an opponent's head; they are almost physical brutalities; there is nothing clever or funny about them. In such a society as this Parisian society of the years '87, '88, '89, '90, he must have been at a continual disadvantage; and at a disadvantage which he felt keenly, but which he felt, also, that any remarkable piece of Alfierism which would have moved Italy to admiration, such as glaring, or stalking off in silence, or punching a man's head, could only increase. To feel himself at a disadvantage on account of his very virtues, and with people whom those virtues did not impress, must have been most intolerable to a man as vain and self-conscious as Alfieri, and to this was added the sense that, from mere ignorance of the language (the language whose nobility, as contrasted with the "low, plebeian, nasal disgustingness" of French, he so often descanted on) in which he wrote, it was quite impossible for these people to be reduced to their right place and right mind by the crushing superiority of his dramatic genius. He, who hungered and thirsted for glory, what glory could he hope for among all these monkeys of Frenchmen, jabbering and gesticulating about their States-General, their Montgolfier, their St. Pierre, their Condorcet, their Parny, their Necker, who had not even the decent feeling to know Italian, and who bowed and smiled and doubtless mixed him up with Metastasio and Goldoni when introduced by the Countess to so odd a piece of provincialism as an Italian poet. "Does Monsieur write comedies or tragedies?" One fancies one can hear the politely indifferent question put with a charming smile by some powdered and embroidered French wit to Mme. d'Albany in Alfieri's hearing; nay, to Alfieri himself.

Mixed with such meaner, though unconscious motives for dissatisfaction, must have been the sense, intolerable to a man like Alfieri, of the horrid and grotesque jumble of good and bad, of real and false, not merely in the revolutionary movement itself, but in all these men of the *ancien régime* who initiated it. Alfieri conceived liberty from the purely antique, or, if you prefer, pseudo-antique, point of view; it was to him the final cause of the world; the aim of all struggles; to be free was the one and only desideratum, to be master of one's own thoughts, actions, and words, merely for the sake of such mastery. The practical advantages of liberty entirely escaped him, as did the practical disadvantages of tyranny; nay, one can almost imagine that had liberty involved absolute misery for all men, and tyranny absolute happiness, Alfieri would have chosen liberty. To this pseudo-Roman and intensely patrician stoic, who had never known privation or injustice towards himself, and scarcely noticed it towards others, the humanitarian, the philanthropic movement, characteristic of the eighteenth century, and which was the strong impulse of the revolution, was absolutely incomprehensible. Alfieri was, in the sense of certain ancients, a hard-hearted man, indifferent, blind and deaf to suffering. That a man of education and mind, a gentleman, should have to sweep the ground with his hat on the passage of another man, because that other happened to wear a ribbon and a star; that he should be liable to exile, to imprisonment, for a truthful statement of his opinion: these were to Alfieri the insupportable things of tyranny. But that a man in wooden shoes and a torn smock frock, sleeping between the pigs and the cows on the damp clay floor, eating bread mainly composed of straw, should have all the profits of his hard labour taken from him in taxes, while another man, a splendid gentleman covered over with gold, riding over acres of his land with his hounds, or a fat priest dressed in silk, snoozing over his Lucullus dinner, should be exempt from taxation and empowered to starve, rob, beat, or hang the peasant: such a thing as this did not fall within the range of Alfieri's feelings. To his mind, for ever wrapped in an intellectual toga, there was no tragedy in mere misery; there was no injustice in mere cruelty, or rather misery, cruelty, nay, all their allied evils, ignorance, brutality, sickness, superstition, vice, were unknown to him. Hence, as I have said, all the philanthropic side of the revolutionary movement was lost to him; just as the defence of Labarre, the vindication of Calas, never disturbed the current of his contempt for Voltaire. So also the abolition of privileges, the secularisation of church property, the equalisation of legal punishment, the abrogation of barbarous laws, the liberation of slaves; all these things, which stirred even the most corrupt and apathetic minds of the late eighteenth century, seemed merely so much declamation to Alfieri. To him, who could conceive no virtues beyond independent truthfulness, such things were mere sentimental trash, mere hypocritical nonsense beneath which base men hid their baseness. And the baseness, unhappily, was there: baseness of absolute corruption, or of scandalous levity, even in the noblest. To Alfieri, a man like Beaumarchais, for all his quick philanthropy, his audacious outspokenness, must have seemed base, with his background of money-jobbing, of dirty diplomatic work, of legal squabbles. How much more such a man as Mirabeau, with his heroic resolution, his heroic kindliness, his whole Titan nature, carous, eaten into by a hundred mean vices. That Mirabeau should have gained his bread writing libels and obscene novels, meant to Alfieri not that a man born in corruption and tainted thereby had, by the force of his genius, by the force of the great humanitarian movement, raised himself as morally high as he had hitherto grovelled morally low; it merely meant that the immaculate name of hero was degraded by a foul writer.

From such figures as these Alfieri turned away in indignant disgust. The great movement of the eighteenth century seemed to him a mere stirring and splashing in a noisome pool, in that *cloaca maxima*, as he had called it.

Already before settling in Paris in 1787, he had written to his Sienese friends that, were it not for the necessity of attending to the printing of his works (to print which permission would not be obtainable in

Italy), he would rather have established himself at Prats, at Colle, at Buonconvento, at any little town of two thousand inhabitants near Florence or Siena. Surrounded by, in daily contact with, some of the noblest minds of the century, nay, of any century, by people like Mme. de Staël, André Chénier, Condorcet, Mirabeau, Alfieri could write, with a sort of bitter pleasure at his own narrow-mindedness: "Now I am among a million of men, and not one of them that is worth Gori's little finger."

I am almost prepared to say that Alfieri really felt as if living in Paris, among such people and at such a moment, was a sort of saintly sacrifice, the crowning heroism of his life, which he made in order to print his books; that he endured the contact of this plague-stricken city, merely because he knew that unless he corrected a certain number of manuscript pages, and revised a certain number of proof-sheets, the world would be defrauded of the great and sovereign antidote to all such baseness as this in the shape of his own complete works.

Writing to his mother towards the end of the year 1788, he mentions contemptuously the excitement and enthusiasm created by the approaching election of the States-General, and adds calmly: "But all these sort of things interest me very little; and I give my attention only to the correction of my proofs, a piece of work with which I am pretty well half through."

XV

ENGLAND

The contradictions in complex and self-contradictory characters like those of the Frenchmen of the early revolution can be easily explained, and, say what we will, must be easily pardoned: rich natures, creatures of impulse, intensely sensitive to external influences, we feel that it is to the very richness of nature, the warmth of impulse, the susceptibility to influence, that we owe not merely these men's virtues but their vices. But the contradictions of the self-righteous are an afflicting spectacle, over which we would fain draw the veil: there is no room in a narrow nature for any flagrant violation of its own ideals to be stuffed away unnoticed in a corner. And now we come to one of the strangest self-contradictions in the history of Mme. d'Albany, that is to say, of her lord and master Alfieri.

The revision and printing of Alfieri's works had been brought to an end; but neither he nor the Countess seems to have contemplated a return to Italy. The fact was that they were both of them retained by money matters. A proportion of Mme. d'Albany's income consisted in the pension which she received from the French Court; and the greater part of Alfieri's income consisted in certain moneys made over to him by his sister as the capital of his life pension, and which he had invested in French funds.

By the year 1791, the French Court and the French funds had got to be very shaky; and those who depended upon them did not dare go to any distance, lest on their return they should find nothing to claim, or no one to claim from. Hence the necessity for Alfieri and the Countess to remain in France, or, at least, hover about near it.

Now, whether the unsettled state of French affairs suggested to Mme. d'Albany, and through her to Alfieri, that it would be wise to see what sort of home, nay, perhaps, what sort of pecuniary assistance, might be found elsewhere, I cannot tell; but this much is certain, that on the 19th May, 1791, Horace Walpole wrote as follows to Miss Barry:—

"The Countess of Albany is not only in England, in London, but at this very moment, I believe, in the palace of St. James; not restored by as rapid a revolution as the French, but, as was observed at supper at

Lady Mount Edgecumbe's, by that topsy-turvihood that characterises the present age. Within these two days the Pope has been burnt at Paris; Mme. du Barry, mistress of Louis Quinze, has dined with the Lord Mayor of London; and the Pretender's widow is presented to the Queen of Great Britain."

That we should have to learn so striking an episode of the journey to England from the letters of a total stranger, who noticed it as a mere piece of gossip, while the memoirs of Alfieri, who accompanied Mme. d'Albany to England, are perfectly silent on the subject, is, to say the least of it, a suspicious circumstance.

As he grew old, Alfieri seems to have lost that power, nay that irresistible desire, of speaking the truth and the whole truth which made him record with burning shame the caress of Pius VI. Perhaps, on the other hand, Alfieri, who, after all, was but a sorry mixture of an ancient Roman and a man of the eighteenth century, thought that a certain amount of baseness and dirt-eating, quite degrading in a man, might be permitted to a woman, even to the lady of his thoughts. And still I cannot help thinking that Alfieri, who could certainly, with his strong will, have prevented the Countess from demeaning herself, and in so far demeaning also his love for her, quietly abetted this step, and then as quietly consigned it to oblivion.

But oblivion did not depend upon registration, or non-registration, in Alfieri's memoirs. The letters of Walpole, the memoirs of Hannah More, the political correspondence collected by Lord Stanhope, furnish abundant detail of this affair. The Countess of Albany was introduced by her relation, or connexion, the young Countess of Aylesbury, and announced by her maiden name of Princess of Stolberg. Horace Walpole's informant, who stood close by, told him that she was "well-dressed, and not at all embarrassed." George III and his sons talked a good deal to her, about her passage, her stay in England, and similar matters; but the princesses none of them said a word; and we hear that Queen Charlotte "looked at her earnestly." The strait-laced wife of George III had probably consented to receive the Pretender's widow, only because this ceremony was a sort of second burial of Charles Edward, a burial of all the claims, the pride of the Stuarts; but she felt presumably no great cordiality towards a woman who had run away from her husband, who was travelling in England with her lover; and who, while affecting royal state in her own house, could crave the honour of being received by the family of the usurper.

Mme. d'Albany was not abashed: she seems to have made up her mind to get all she could out of royal friendliness. She accepted a seat in the King's box at the opera; nay, she accepted a seat at the foot of the throne ("the throne she might once have expected to mount," remarks Hannah More), on the occasion of the King's speech in the House of Lords. It was the 10th of June, the birthday of Prince Charlie; and the woman who sat there so unconcernedly, kept a throne with the British arms in her ante-room, and made her servants address her as a Queen!

What were Alfieri's feelings when Mme. d'Albany came home in her Court toilette, and told him of all these fine doings? The more we try to conceive certain things, the more inconceivable they become: it is like straining to see what may be hidden at the bottom of a very deep well. In the case of Alfieri, I think we may add that the well was empty. Since his illness at Colmar, he had aged in the most extraordinary way: the process of dessication and ossification of his moral nerves and muscles, which, as I have said, was the form that premature decrepitude took in this abnormal man, had begun. The creative power was extinct in him, both as regards his works and himself: there was no possibility of anything new, of any response of this wooden nature to new circumstances. He had attained to the age of forty-two without any particular feelings such as could fit into this present case, and the result was that he probably had no feelings. The Countess of Albany was the ideal woman he had enshrined her as such ages ago, and an ideal woman could not change, could not commit an impropriety, least of all in his eyes. If she had condescended to ridiculous meanness in order to secure for herself an opening in English society, a subsidy from the English Government (apparently already suggested at that time, but granted only many years later) in case of a general break-up of French things; if she had done this, it was no concern of Alfieri: Mme. d'Albany had been patented as the ideal woman. As to him, why should he condescend to think about state receptions, galas, pensions, kings and queens, and similar low things? He had put such vanities behind him long ago.

Alfieri and the Countess made a tour through England, and projected a tour through Scotland. Whether the climate, the manners, the aspect of England and its inhabitants really disappointed the perhaps ideal notions she had formed; or whether, perhaps, she was a little bit put out of sorts by no pension being granted, and by a possible coldness of British matrons towards a widow travelling about with an Italian poet, it is not for me to decide. But her impressions of England, as recorded in a note-book now at the Musée Fabre at Montpellier, are certainly not those of a person who has received a good welcome:

"Although I knew," she says, repeating the stale platitudes (or perhaps the true impressions?) of all foreigners, "that the English were melancholy, I had not imagined that life in their capital would be so to the point which I experienced it. No sort of society, and a quantity of crowds. . . As they spend nine months in the country—the family alone, or with only a very few friends—they like, when they come to town, to throw themselves into the vortex. Women are never at home. The whole early part of the day, which begins at two (for, going to bed at four in the morning, they rise only at mid-day), is spent in visits and exercise, for the English require, and their climate absolutely necessitates, a great deal of exercise. The coal smoke, the constant absence of sunshine, the heavy food and drink, make movement a necessity to them. . . If England had an oppressive Government, this country and its inhabitants would be the lowest in the universe: a bad climate, bad soil, hence no sort of taste; it is only the excellence of the political constitution which renders it inhabitable. The nation is melancholy, without any imagination, even without wit; the dominant characteristic is a desire for money."

The same note as that even of such a man as Taine. The almost morbid love of beauty which a civilisation, whose outward expression are the lines and lines of black boxes, with slits for doors and windows of Bloomsbury, produced in men like Coleridge, Blake, and Turner, naturally escaped Mme. d'Albany; but the second great rebellion of imagination and love of beauty, the rebellion led by Madox Brown and Morris, and Rossetti and Burne Jones, escaped Taine. But of all the things which most offended this quasi-Queen of England in our civilisation, the social arrangements did so most of all. With the instinct of a woman who has lived a by no means regular life in the midst of a society far worse than herself, with the instinct of one of those strange pseudo-French Continental mongrels with whom age always brings cynicism, she tries to account for the virtue of Englishwomen by accidental, and often rather nasty, necessities. Mme. d'Albany writes with the freedom and precision of a Continental woman of the world of eighty years ago; and her remarks lose too much or gain too much by translation into our chaster language. "The charm of intimate society," she winds up, conscious of the charms of her own little salon full of clever men and pretty women all well-acquainted with each other—"the charm of intimate society is unknown in England."

In short, the sooner England be quitted, the better. Political, or rather financial circumstances—that is to say, the frightful worthlessness of French money (and Alfieri's and her money came mainly from France), made a return to Paris urgent.

An incident, as curious perhaps as that of Mme. d'Albany's presentation at Court, but which, unlike that, Alfieri has not thought fit to suppress, marked their departure from England. As Alfieri, who had preceded the Countess by a few minutes to see whether the luggage had been properly stored on the ship at Dover, turned to go and meet her, his eyes suddenly fell with a start of recognition upon a woman standing on the landing-place. She was not young, but still very handsome, as some of us may know her from Gainsborough's portrait; and she was no other than Penelope Lady Ligonier, for whom Alfieri had been so mad twenty years before, for whom he had fought his famous duel in St. James' Park, and got himself disgracefully mixed up in a peculiarly disgraceful divorce suit. He had several times inquired after her, and always in vain; and now he would scarcely have believed his eyes had his former mistress not given him a smile of recognition. Alfieri was terribly upset. The sight of this ghost from out of a disgraceful past, coming to haunt what he considered a dignified present, seems fairly to have terrified him; he ran back into the ship and dared not go to meet Mme. d'Albany, lest in so doing he should meet Lady Ligonier. Presently, Mme. d'Albany came on board. With the indifference of a woman of the world, of that easy-goingness which was rapidly effacing in her the romantic victim of Charles Edward, she told Alfieri that the friends who had escorted her to the ship (and who appear to have perfectly understood the temper of the Countess) had pointed out his former flame and entertained her with a brief biography of her predecessor in Alfieri's heart. Mme. d'Albany took it all as a matter of course: she was probably no longer at all in love with Alfieri, but she admired his genius and character as much and more than ever; and was probably beginning to develop a certain good-natured, half-motherly acquiescence in his eccentricities, such as women who have suffered much, and grown stout and strong, and cynically optimistic now that suffering is over, are apt to develop towards people accustomed to resort to them, like sick children, in all their ups and downs of temper.

"Between us," says Alfieri, "there was never any falsehood, or reticence, or coolness, or quarrel";—and, indeed, when a woman, such as Mme. d'Albany must have been at the age of forty, has once determined to adore and humour a particular individual in every single possible thing, all such painful results of more sensitive passion naturally become unnecessary. If Mme. d'Albany merely smiled over bygone follies, Alfieri had been put into great agitation by the sight of Lady Ligonier. From Calais he sent her a letter, of which no copy has been preserved, but which, according to his account, "was full, not indeed of love, but of a deep and sincere emotion at seeing her still leading a wandering life very unsuited to her birth and position; and of pain in thinking that I, although innocently (that "although innocently", on the part of a man who had been the cause of her scandalous downfall, is perfectly charming in its simple revelation of Continental morals), might have been the cause or the pretext thereof."

Lady Ligonier's answer came to hand in Brussels. Written in bad French, it answered Alfieri's tragic grandiloquence with a cold civility, which shows how deeply his magnanimous compassion had wounded a woman who felt herself to be no more really corrupt than he.

"Monsieur," so runs the letter, "you could not doubt that the expression of your remembrance of me, and of the interest which you kindly take in my lot, would be duly appreciated and received gratefully by me; the more especially as I cannot consider you as the cause of my unhappiness, since I am not unhappy, although the uprightness of your soul makes you fear that I am. You were, on the contrary, the agent of my liberation from a world for which I was in no way suited, and which I have not for a moment regretted. . . I am in the enjoyment of perfect health, increased by liberty and peace of mind. I seek the society only of simple and virtuous persons without pretensions either to particular genius or to particular learning; and besides such society I entertain myself with books, drawing, music, &c. But what constitutes the basis of real happiness and satisfaction is the friendship and unalterable love of a brother whom I have always loved more than the whole world, and who possesses the best of hearts." "I hear," goes on Lady Ligonier, after a few compliments on Alfieri's literary fame, "that you are attached to the Princess with whom you are travelling, whose amiable and clever physiognomy seems indeed formed for the happiness of a soul as sensitive and delicate as yours. I am also told that she is afraid of you: I recognise you there. Without wishing, or perhaps even knowing it, you have an irresistible ascendancy over all who are attached to you."

Was it this disrespectful hint concerning what he wished the world to consider as his ideal love for Mme. d'Albany, or was it Lady Ligonier's determination to let him know that desertion by him had made her neither more disreputable nor more unhappy than before, I cannot tell; but certain it is that something in this letter appears to have put Alfieri, who had not objected to Mme. d'Albany's mean behaviour towards George III, into a condition of ruffled virtue and dignity.

"I copy this letter," he writes in his memoirs, "in order to give an idea of this woman's eccentric and obstinately evilly-inclined character."

Did it never occur to Alfieri that his own character, whose faults during youth he so keenly appreciated, was not improving with years?

XVI

THE MISOGALLO

A lfieri and Madame d'Albany were scarcely back in Paris, and settled in a new house, when the disorders in Paris and the movements of the Imperial troops on the frontier began to make the situation of foreigners difficult and dangerous. The storming of the Tuileries, the great slaughter of the 10th August 1792, admonished them to sacrifice everything to their safety. With considerable difficulty a passport for the Countess had been obtained from the Swedish Minister, one for Alfieri from the Venetian Resident (almost the only diplomatic representatives, says Alfieri, who still remained to that ghost of a king), and a passport for each of them and for each of their servants from their communal section. Departure was fixed for the 20th August, but Alfieri's black presentiments hastened it to the 18th. Arrived at the Barrière Blanche, on the road to Calais, passports were examined by two or three soldiers of the National Guard, and the gates were on the point of being opened to let the two heavily-loaded carriages pass, when suddenly, from out of a neighbouring pot-house, rushed some twenty-five or thirty ruffians, ragged, drunken, and furious. They surrounded the carriages, yelling that all the rich were running away and leaving them to starve without work; and a crowd rapidly formed round them and the National Guards, who wanted the travellers to be permitted to pass on. Alfieri jumps out of the carriage, brandishing his seven passports, and throws himself, a long, lean, red-haired man, fiercely gesticulating and yelling at the top of his voice, among the crowd, forcing this man and that to read the passports, crying frantically, "Look! Listen! Name Alfieri. Italian and not French! Tall, thin, pale, red-haired; that is I; look at me. I have my passport! We have our passports all in order from the proper authorities! We want to pass; and, by God! we will pass!"

After half an hour of this altercation, with voices issuing from the crowd, "Burn the carriages!" "Throw stones at them!" "They are running away, they are noble and rich; take them to the Hotel de Ville to be judged!" at last Alfieri's vociferations and gesticulations wearied even the Paris mob, the crowd became quieter, the National Guards gave the sign for departure, and Alfieri, jumping into the carriage where

Mme. d'Albany was sitting more dead than alive, shouted to the postillions to gallop off.

At a country house near Mons, belonging to the Countess of Albany's sister, the fugitives received the frightful news of the September massacres; of those men and women driven, like beasts into an arena, down the prison-stairs into the prison yard, to fall, hacked to pieces by the bayonets and sabres and pikes of Maillard's amateur executioners, on to the blood-soaked mattresses, while the people of Paris, morally divided on separate benches, the gentlemen here, the ladies there, sat and looked on; of those men and women many had frequented the salon of the Rue de Bourgoyne, had chatted and laughed, only a few weeks back, with Alfieri and the Countess; amongst those men and women Alfieri and the Countess might themselves easily have been, had the ruffians of the Barrière Blanche dragged them back to their house, where an order to arrest Mme. d'Albany arrived two days later, that very 20th August which had originally been fixed for their departure. The thought of this narrow escape turned the recollection of that scene at the Barrière Blanche into a perfect nightmare, which focussed, so to speak, all the frenzied horror conceived by Alfieri for the French Revolution, for the "Tiger-Apes" of France.

By November Alfieri and Mme. d'Albany were in Florence, safe; but established in a miserable inn, without their furniture, their horses, their books; all left in Paris; nay, almost without the necessary clothes, and with very little money. From the dirty inn they migrated into rather unseemly furnished lodgings, and finally, after some debating about Siena and inquiring whether a house might not be had there on the promenade of the Lizza, they settled down in the house, one of a number formerly belonging to the Gianfigliazzi family, on the Lung Arno, close to the Ponte Santa Trinita, in Florence. The situation is one of the most delightful in Florence: across the narrow quay the windows look almost sheer down into the river, sparkling with a hundred facets in the spring and summer sunlight, cut by the deep shadows of the old bridges, to where it is lost to sight between the tall poplars by the Greve mouth and the ilexes and elms of the Cascine, closed in by the pale blue peaks of the Carrara Alps; or else, in autumn and winter, scarcely moving, a mass of dark-greens and browns, wonderfully veined, like some strange oriental jasper, with transparent violet streakings, and above which arise, veiled, half washed out by mist, the old corbelled houses, the church-steeples and roofs, the tiers and tiers of pine and ilex plumes on the hill opposite.

For a moment, with the full luminousness of the Tuscan sky once more in his eyes, and the guttural strength of the Tuscan language once more in his ears, Alfieri seems to have been delighted. But his cheerfulness was not of long duration. Ever since his great illness at Colmar, Alfieri had, I feel persuaded, become virtually an old man; his strength and spirits were impaired, and the strange morose depression of his half-fructified youth seemed to return. Coming at that moment, the disappointment, the terror, the horror of the French Revolution became, so to speak, part of a moral illness which lasted to his death. Alfieri was not a tender-hearted nor a humane man; had he been, he would have felt more sympathy than he did with the beginning of the great movement, with the strivings after reform which preceded it; he had, on the contrary, the sort of cold continuous rage, the ruthless self-righteousness and cut-and-dryness which would have made him, had he been a Frenchman, a terrorist of the most dreadful type; a regular routinist in extermination of corrupt people. Hence I cannot believe that, much as he may have been shocked by the news of the September massacres, of the *grandes fournées* which preceded Thermidor, and much as he may have been distressed by Mme. d'Albany's anxiety and grief for so many friends who lost their property or life, Alfieri was the man to be driven mad by the mere thought of bloodshed. But Alfieri had, ever since his earliest youth, made liberty his goddess, and the worship of liberty his special religion and mission. That such a religion and mission, to which he had devoted himself in a time and country when and where no one else dreamed of anything of the sort, should suddenly become, and without the smallest agency of his, the religion and mission of the very nation and people whom he instinctively abhorred from the depths of his soul; that liberty, which he alone was to teach men to desire, should be the fashionable craze, mixed up with science, philanthropy, sentiment, and everything he hated most in the French, this was already a pain that gnawed silently into Alfieri's soul. But when liberty was, as it were, dragged out of his own little private temple, where he adored and hymned it, decked out in patrician dignity of Plutarch and Livy, and carried about, dressed in the garb of a Paris fish-wife, a red cotton night-cap on her head, by a tattered, filthy, drunken, blood-stained crew of *sansculottes*, nay, worse, rolled along on a triumphal car by an assembly of lawyers and doctors and ex-priests and journalists— when liberty, which had been to him antique and aristocratic, became modern and democratic; when the whole of France had turned into a blood-reeking and streaming temple of this Moloch goddess, then a sort of moral abscess, long growing unnoticed, seemed to burst within Alfieri's soul, and a process of slow moral blood-poisoning to begin.

The Reign of Terror came to an end, the reaction of Thermidor set in; but this was nothing to Alfieri, for, whereas the unspeakable profanation of what was his own personal and quasi-private property, liberty, had hitherto been limited to France, it now spread, a frightful invading abomination, with the armies of the Directory all over the world; nay, to Italy itself.

It was as an expression, an eternal, immortal expression, the severest conceivable retribution, Alfieri sincerely thought, of this rage, all the stronger as there entered into it the petty personal vanity as well as the noble abstract feeling of the man—it was as an expression of this gallophobia that Alfieri composed his famous but little-read *Misogallo*. This collection of prose arguments and vituperations and versified epigrams, all larded and loaded with quotations from all the Latin and Greek authors whom Alfieri was busy spelling out, does certainly contain many things which, old as they are, strike even us with the force of living contempt and indignation. Nay, even including its most stupid and dullest violent parts, we can sympathise with its bitterness and violence, when we think of the frightful deeds of blood which, talking heroically of justice and liberty, France had been committing; of the miserable series of petty rapines and extortions which, talking patronisingly of the Greeks and Romans, the French nation was practising upon the Italians whom it had come to liberate. That such feeling should be elicited was natural enough. But we feel, as we turn over the pages of the *Misogallo*, and collate with its epigrams a certain passage in Alfieri's memoirs and letters, that when we meet it in this particular man, in this hard, savage, narrow, pedantic doctrinaire, whose very magnanimity is vanity and egotism, we can no longer sympathise with the hatred of the French, which in juster and more modest men, as for instance Carlo Botta, invariably elicits our sympathy. Much as we dislike the republican French who descended into Italy, the *Misogallo* makes us like Alfieri even less. Whether this revolution, despite the oceans of blood which it shed, might not be bringing a great and lasting benefit to mankind by sweeping away the hundred and one obstacles which impeded social progress; whether this French invasion, despite the money which it extorted, the statues and pictures which it stole, the miserable high-flown lies which it told, might not be doing Italy a great service in accustoming it to modern institutions, in training it to warfare, in ridding it of a brood of inept little tyrants: such questions did not occur to Alfieri, for whom liberty meant everything, progress and improvement nothing. As the century drew to a close, and the futility of so many vaunted reforms, the hollowness of so many promises, became apparent to the Italians with the shameful treaty which gave Venice, liberated of her oligarchy, to Austria, all the nobler men of the day, Pindemonti, Botta, Foscolo, and the crowds of nameless patriotic youths who filled the universities, were seized by a terrible soul-sickness; everything seemed to have given way, each course was as bad as the other, and Italy seemed destined to servitude and indignity, whether under her new masters the French, or under her old masters the Austrians and Bourbons and priests. But the feelings of Alfieri were not of this kind; he was not torn by patriotism; he was simply pushed into sympathy with the tyrannies which he had so hated by the intolerable pain of finding that the liberty which he had preached was being propagandised by the nation and the class of society which he detested most.

Such Alfieri appears to me, and such I think he must appear to everyone who conscientiously studies the extraordinary manner in which this apostle of liberty came to preach in favour of despotism. But in his own eyes, and in the eyes of the Countess of Albany, Alfieri doubtless found abundant arguments to prove himself perfectly logical and magnanimous. This French Revolution was merely a revolt of slaves; and what tyranny could be more odious than the tyranny of those whom nature had fitted only for slavery? What are the French? "The French," answers one of the epigrams of the *Misogallo*, "have always been puppets; formerly puppets in powder, now stinking and blood-stained puppets." "We indeed are slaves," says another epigram, "but at least indignant slaves" (a statement which the whole history of Italy in the nineties goes to disprove); "not, as you Gauls always have been and always will be, slaves applauding power whatever it be." The nasal and guttural pronunciation of the French language, the bare existence of such a word as *quatrain*, is enough to prove to Alfieri that the French can never know true liberty. Alfieri, who had looked the *ancien régime* more than once in the face, actually persuaded himself that, as he writes, "the frightful French mob robbed and slaughtered the upper classes because those upper classes had always treated it too kindly." Alfieri actually got to believe these things. He would, had power been put in his hands, have headed a counter revolution and exterminated as many people again as the republicans had exterminated. Power not being in his hands, he hastened to do what seemed to him a vital matter to all Europe, a sort of fatal thrust to France; he solemnly recanted all his former writings in favour of revolutions and republics. He, who had witnessed the taking of the Bastille and sung it in an ode, deliberately wrote as follows: "The famous day of the 14th July 1789 crowned the victorious iniquity (of the people). Not understanding at that time the nature of these slaves, I dishonoured my pen by writing an ode on the taking of the Bastille." Surely, if we admit that to see liberty degraded by its association with revolutionary horrors must have been unbearably bitter to the nobler portion of Alfieri's nature, we must admit that to see Alfieri himself, Alfieri so proud of his former ferocious love of liberty, turned into a mere ranting renegade, is an unendurable spectacle also; we should like to wash our hands of him as he tried to wash his hands of the Revolution.

All this political atrabiliousness did not improve Alfieri's temper; and could not have made it easier or more agreeable to live with him. The Countess of Albany naturally disliked the Revolution and the French, after all the grief and inconvenience which she owed them; she naturally, also, disliked everything that Alfieri disliked. Still, I cannot help fancying that this woman, far more intellectual than passionate, and growing more indifferent, more easy-going, more half-optimistically, half-cynically charitable towards the world with every year that saw her grow fat, and plain, and dowdy,—I cannot help fancying that the Countess of Albany must have got to listen to Alfieri's misogallic furies much as she might have listened to his groans had he been afflicted with gout or the toothache, sympathising with the pain, but just a little weary of its expression. She must also, at times, have compared the little company of select provincial notabilities, illustrious people never known beyond their town and their lifetime, which she collected about herself and Alfieri in the house by the Arno, with the brilliant society which had assembled in her hotel in Paris. To her, who was, after all, not Italian, but French by education and temper, and who had been steeped anew in French ideas and habits, this small fry of Italian literature, professional and pedantic, able to discuss and (alas! but too able) to hold forth, but absolutely unable to talk, to *causer* in the French sense, must have become rather oppressive. She and Alfieri were both growing elderly, and the hearth by which they were seated, alone, childless, with nothing but the ghost of their former passion, the ghost of their former ideal, to keep them company, was on the whole very bleak and cheerless. Alfieri, working off his over-excitement in a system of tremendous self-education, sitting for the greater part of the day poring over Latin and Greek and Hebrew grammars, and exercises and annotated editions, till he was so exhausted that he could scarcely digest his dinner; the Countess killing the endless days reading new books of philosophy, of poetry, of fiction, anything and everything that came to hand, writing piles and piles of letters to every person of her acquaintance; this double existence of bored and overworked dreariness, was this the equivalent of marriage? was this the realisation of ideal love?

But there were things to confirm Mme. d'Albany in that easy-going indifferentism which replaced passion and suffering in this fat, kindly, intellectual woman of forty; things which, as they might have made other women weep, probably made this woman do what in its way was just as sad—smile.

Alfieri had always had what, to us, may seem very strange notions on the subject of love, but which were not strange when we consider the times and nation in general, and the man in particular. After the various love manias which preceded his meeting with Mme. d'Albany, he had determined, as he tells us, to save his peace of mind and dignity by refusing to fall in love with women of respectable position. The Countess of Albany, by enchaining him in the bonds of what he called "worthy love," had saved him from any chance of fresh follies with these alarming "virtuous women." But follies with women of less respectable position and less obvious virtue appear to have presented no fear of degradation to Alfieri's mind. And now, late on in the nineties, when Mme. d'Albany was rapidly growing plain and stout and elderly, and he was getting into the systematic habit of regarding her less in her reality than in the ideal image which he had arranged in his mind; now, when he was writing the autobiography where the Countess figured as his Beatrice, and when he was composing the Latin epitaphs which were to unite his tomb with that of the woman "a Victorio Alferio, ultra resomnia dilecta," just at this time Alfieri appears to have returned to those flirtations with women neither respectable nor virtuous which seemed to him so morally safe to indulge in. A very strange note, preserved at Siena, to a "Nina padrona mia dilettissima," shows that the memory of Gori and the friendship of Gori's friends were not the only things which attracted him ever and anon from Florence to Siena. A collection of wretched bouts-rimés and burlesque doggrel, written at Florence in a house which Mme. d'Albany could not enter, and in the company of women whom Mme. d'Albany could not receive, and among which is a sonnet in which Alfieri explains his condescension in joining in these poetical exercises of the demi-monde by an allusion to Hercules and Omphale, shows that Alfieri frequented in Florence other society besides that which crowded round his lady in Casa Gianfigliazzi.

Mme. d'Albany was far too shrewd and far too worldly not to see all this; and Alfieri was far too open and cynical to attempt to hide it. Mme. d'Albany, having her praises and his love read to her in innumerable sonnets, in the autobiography and in the epitaphs, probably merely smiled; she was a woman of the eighteenth century, a foreigner, an easy-going woman, and had learned to consider such escapades as these as an inevitable part of matrimony or quasi-matrimony. But, for all her worldly philosophy, did she never feel a vague craving, a void, as she sat in that big empty house reading her books while Alfieri was studying his Greek, a vague desire to have what consoles other women for coldness or infidelity, a son or a daughter, a normal object of devotion, something besides Alfieri, and which she could love whether deserving or not; something besides Alfieri's glory, in which she could take an interest whether other people did or did not agree? Such a connection as hers with Alfieri may have had an attraction of romance, of poetry, connected with its very illegitimacy, its very negation of normal domestic life, as long as both she and Alfieri were young and passionately in love; but where was the romance, the poetry now, and where was the humdrum married woman's happiness, at whose expense that romance, that poetry, had been bought?

Mme. d'Albany, if I may judge by the enormous piles of her letters which I have myself seen, and by the report of my friend Signor Mario Pratesi, who has examined another huge collection for my benefit, was getting to make herself a sort of half-vegetating intellectual life, reading so many hours a day, writing letters so many more hours; taking the quite unenthusiastic, business-like interest in literature and politics of a woman whose life is very empty, and, it seems to me, from the tone of her letters, growing daily more indifferent to life, more desultory, more cynical, more misanthropic and tittle-tattling. And Alfieri, meanwhile, was growing more unsociable, more misanthropic, more violent in temper, hanging a printed card stating that he wished no visits (one such is preserved in the library at Florence) in the hall, pursuing and flogging street-boys because they splashed his stockings by playing in the puddles; insulting Ginguené and General Miollis when they attempted to be civil; groaning over the victories of the French, rejoicing over the brutal massacres by the priest-hounded Tuscan populace; going to Florence (when they were spending the summer in a villa) for the pleasure of seeing the Austrian troops enter, and of witnessing (as Gino Capponi records) the French prisoners or Frenchly-inclined Florentines being pilloried and tortured by the anti-revolutionary mob. Besides such demonstrations of an unamiable disposition as these, working with the fury of an alchemist, and, perhaps, taking a holiday at that house where the doggrel verses were written. The Countess of Albany, who had been so horribly unhappy with her legitimate husband, must have been rather dreary of soul with her world-authorised lover.

It was at this moment, as she sat, an idle, desultory, neither happy nor unhappy woman, rapidly growing old, watching the century draw to a close amid chaos and misery,—it was at this moment that an eccentric English prelate, Lord Bristol, Bishop of Derry, introduced at the house on the Lung Arno a friend of his, a French painter, a former pupil of David, and who had won the *Prix de Rome*, by name François Xavier Fabre. M. Fabre was French, but he was a royalist; he hated the Revolution; he had settled in Italy; and, in consideration of this, he was tolerated by Alfieri. To Mme. d'Albany, on the other hand, the fact of Fabre being French must secretly have been a great recommendation. French in language, habits, mode of thought, French in heart, cut off, as it seemed, for ever from Paris and Parisian society, cooped up among this pedantic small fry of Florentines, listening all day to Alfieri's tirades against the French nation, the French reforms, the French philosophy, the French language, the French everything, the poor woman must have heartily enjoyed an hour's chat in good French with a real Frenchman, a Frenchman who, for all Alfieri might say, was really French; she must have enjoyed talking about his work, his pictures, about everything and anything that was not Alfieri's Greek, or Alfieri's Hebrew, or Alfieri's tragedies, or comedies or satires. Alfieri was a great genius and a great man; and she loved, or imagined she loved, Alfieri like her very soul. But still—still, it was somehow a relief when young Fabre, with his regular south-of-

France face, his rather mocking and cynical French expression, his easy French talk, came to give her a painting lesson while Alfieri was pacing up and down translating Homer and Pindar with the help of a lexicon.

XVII

CASA GIANFIGLIAZZI

Thus things jogged on. Occasionally a grand performance of one of Alfieri's plays enlivened the house on the Lung Arno. A room was filled with chairs, arranged with curtains, and a select company invited to see the poet (for by this respectful title he appears always to have been mentioned) play Saul or Creon, to his own admiration, but apparently less so to that of his guests. Occasionally, also, Alfieri and Mme. d'Albany would go for a few days to Siena to enjoy the conversation of a little knot of friends of their dead friend Gori; a certain Cavaliere Bianchi, a certain Canon Ansano Luti, a certain Alessandro Cerretani, and one or two others, who met in the house of a charming and intellectual woman, Teresa Regoli, daughter of a Sienese shopkeeper, married to another shopkeeper, called Mocenni, and who was one of Mme. d'Albany's most intimate friends. Occasionally, also, some of these would come for a jaunt to Florence, when Alfieri and the Countess moved heaven and earth (recollecting their own aversion to husbands) that the *Grumbler*, as Signor Mocenni was familiarly called, should be left behind, and *la chère* Thérèse come accompanied (in characteristic Italian eighteenth-century fashion) only by her children and by her *cavaliere servente*, Mario Bianchi. These were the small excitements in this curious double life of more than married routine. Alfieri, who, as he was getting old and weak in health, was growing only the more furiously active and rigidly disciplinarian, had determined to learn Greek, to read all the great Greek authors; and worked away with terrific ardour at this school-boy work, crowning his efforts with a self-constituted Order of Homer, of which he himself was the sole founder and sole member. He was, also, having finally despatched the sacramental number of tragedies, working at an equally sacramental number of satires and comedies, absolutely unconscious of his complete deficiency in both these styles, and persuaded that he owed it to his nation to set them on the right road in comedy and satire, as he had set them on the right road in tragedy.

A ridiculous man! Not so. I have spoken many hard words against Alfieri; and I repeat that he seems to me to have often fallen short, betrayed by his century, his vanity, his narrowness and hardness of temper, even of the ideal which he had set up for himself. But I would not have it supposed that I do not see the greatness of that ideal, and the nobleness of the reality out of which it arose. That Alfieri, a strange mixture of the passionate man of spontaneous action, and of the self-manipulating, idealising *poseur*, should have fallen short of his own ideals, is perhaps the one pathetic circumstance of his life; the one dash of suffering and failure which makes this heroic man a hero. Alfieri did not probably suspect wherein he fell short of his own ideal; he did not, could not see that his faults were narrowness of nature, and incompleteness, meanness of conception, for, if he had, he would have ceased to be narrow and ceased to be mean. But Alfieri knew that there was something very wrong about himself, he felt a deficiency, a jar in his own soul; he felt, as he describes in the famous sonnet at the back of Fabre's portrait of him, that he did not know whether he was noble or base, whether he was Achilles or Thersites.

"*Uom, sei tu grande o vile? Mori, il saprai.*" ("Man, art thou noble or base? Die, and thou shalt know it.") Thus wrote Alfieri, making, as usual, fame the arbiter of his worth; and showing, even in the moment of seeking for truth about himself, how utterly and hopelessly impossible it was for him to feel it. Mean and great; both, I think, at once. But of the meanness, the narrowness of nature, the want of resonance of fibre, the insufficiency of moral vitality in so many things; of Alfieri's vanity, intolerance, injustice, indifference, hardness; of all these peculiarities which make the real man repulsive, the ideal man unattractive, to us, I have said more than enough, and when we have said all this, Alfieri still remains, for all his vanity, selfishness, meanness, narrow-mindedness, a man of grander proportions, of finer materials, nay, even of nobler moral shape, than the vast majority of men superior to him in all these points. Let us look at him in those last decaying years, at those studies which have seemed to us absurd: self-important, pedantic, almost monomaniac; or brooding over those feelings which were, doubtless, selfish, morbid; let us look at him, for, despite all his faults, he is fine. Fine in indomitable energy, in irrepressible passion. Alfieri was fifty; he was tormented by gout; his health was rapidly sinking; but the sense of weakness only made him more resolute to finish the work which (however mistakenly) he thought it his duty to leave completed; more determined that, having lived for so many years a dunce, he would go down to the grave cleansed of the stain of ignorance, having read and appreciated as much of the great writers of antiquity as any man who had had a well-trained youth, a studious manhood. Soon after his great illness (which, I believe, changed him so much for the worse by hastening premature old age) at Colmar, he had written to his friends at Siena that he had very nearly been made a fool of by Death; but that, having escaped, he intended, by hurrying his work, to make a fool of Death instead. And in 1801 he wrote in his memorandum-book: "Health giving way year by year; whence, hurrying to finish my six comedies, I make it decidedly worse."

Soon after, as Mme. d'Albany later informed his friend Caluso, Alfieri, finding that his digestion had become so bad as to produce inability to work after meals, began systematically to diminish his already extremely sober allowance of food; while, at the same time, he did not diminish the exercise, walking, riding, and driving, which he found necessary to keep himself in spirits. Knowing that death could not be far ahead, and accustomed since his youth to think that his life ought not to extend over sixty years, Alfieri was calmly and deliberately walking to meet Death.

Calmly and deliberately; but not heartlessly. Engrossed in his studies, devoted to his own glory as he was, he was still full of a kind of mental passion for Mme. d'Albany. He was unfaithful to her for the sake of low women, he was neglectful of her for the sake of his work; he did not, perhaps, receive much pleasure from this stout, plain, prosaic lady (like one of Rubens's women grown old, as Lamartine later described her) whom he left to her letter-writing, her reading of Kant, of La Harpe, of Shakespeare, of Lessing; to her painting lessons, and long discussions on art with Monsieur Fabre. The woman whose presence, no longer exciting, was doubtless a matter of indifference to him. But, nevertheless, it seems to me probable that Alfieri never wrote more completely from his heart than when, composing the epitaph of the Countess, he said of Mme. d'Albany that she had been loved by him more than anything on earth, and held almost as a mortal divinity. "A Victorio Alferio. . . ultra res omnes dilecta, et quasi mortale numen ab ipso constanter habita et observata." For a thought begins about the year 1796 to recur throughout Alfieri's letters and sonnets, and whenever he mentions the Countess in his autobiography; a thought too terrible not to be genuine: he or his beloved must die first; one or the other must have the horror of remaining alone, widowed of all interest on earth. How constantly this idea haunted him, and with what painful vividness, is apparent from a letter which I shall translate almost *in extenso*; as, together with those few words which I have quoted about Gori's death, it shows the passionate tenderness that was hidden, like some aromatic herb beneath the Alpine snow, under the harsh exterior of Alfieri.

The letter is to Mme. Teresa Mocenni at Siena, and relates to the death of Mario Bianchi, who had long been her devoted *cavaliere servente*. "Your letter," writes Alfieri, "breaks my heart. I feel the complete horror of a situation which it gives me the shivers merely to think may be my situation one day or other; and oh! how much worse would it not be for me, living alone, isolated from everyone, closed up in myself. O God! I hope I may not be the survivor, and yet how can I wish that my better self (*la parte migliore di me stesso*) should endure a situation which I myself could never have the courage to endure? These are frightful things. I think about them very often, and sometimes I write some bad rhymes about them to ease my mind; but I never can get accustomed either to the thought of remaining alone, nor to that of leaving my lady." "Some opinions," he goes on—and this hankering after Christianity on the part of a man who had lived in eighteenth-century disbelief seems to bear out what Mme. d'Albany told the late Gino Capponi, that had Alfieri lived much longer he would have died telling his rosary,—"some opinions are more useful and give more satisfaction than others to a well-constituted heart. Thus, it does our affection much more good to believe that our Mario (Bianchi) is united to Candido (another dead friend) and to Gori, that they are talking and thinking about us, and that we shall meet them all some day, than to believe that they are all of them reduced to a handful of ashes. If such a belief as the first is repugnant to physics and to mathematical evidence, it is not, therefore, to be despised. The principal advantage and honour of mankind is that it can feel, and science teaches us how not to feel. Long live, therefore, ignorance and poetry, and let us accept the imaginary as the true. Man subsists upon love; love makes him a god: for I call *God* an intensely felt love, and I call dogs, or French, which comes to the same, the frozen philosophisers who are moved only by the fact that two and two make four."

Alfieri's secret desire that he might not survive his beloved was fulfilled sooner, perhaps, than he expected. The eccentric figure, the tall, gaunt man, thin and pale as a ghost, with flying red hair and flying scarlet cloak, driving the well-known phaeton, or sauntering moodily along the Lung Arno and through the Boboli gardens, was soon to be seen no more. As the year 1803 wore on he felt himself hard pressed by the gout; he ate less and less, he took an enormous amount of foot exercise; he worked madly at his memoirs, his comedies, his translations, he felt almost constantly fatigued and depressed. On the 3rd October 1803, after his usual morning's work, he went out for a drive in his phaeton; but a strange and excessive cold, despite the still summer weather, forced him to alight and to try and warm himself by walking. Walking brought on violent internal pains, and he returned home with the fever on him. The next day he rose and dressed, but he was unable to eat or work, and fell into a long drowse; the next day after that he again tried to take a walk, but returned with frightful pains. He refused to go to bed except at night, and tore off the mustard plaisters which the doctors had placed on his feet, lest the blisters should prevent his walking; dying, he would still not be a sick man. The night of the 8th he was unable to sleep, and talked a great deal to the Countess, seated by his bedside, about his work, and repeated part of Hesiod in Greek to her. Accustomed for months to the idea of death, he does not seem to have guessed that it was near at hand. But the news that he was dying spread through Florence. A Piedmontese lady—strangely enough a niece of that Marchesa de Prié opposite to whose windows Alfieri had renewed the device of Ulysses and the sirens by being tied to a chair—hastened to a learned and eccentric priest, a Padre Canovai, entreating him to run and offer the dying poet the consolations of religion. Canovai, knowing that both Alfieri and Mme. d'Albany were unbelievers, stoutly refused; but later on, seized with remorse, he hurried to the house on the Lung Arno. Admitted into the sick room, he came just in time to see Alfieri, who had got up during a momentary absence of Mme. d'Albany, rise from his arm-chair, lean against his bed, and, without agony or effort, unconscious "like a bird," says the Countess, give up the ghost. It was between nine and ten of the morning of the 9th October 1803. Vittorio Alfieri was in his fifty-fifth year.

The Abate di Caluso, the greatest friend he had, after Gori, was summoned from Turin to console the Countess and put all papers in order. Alfieri's will, made out in 1799, left all his books and Mss., and whatever small property he possessed, to the Countess Louise d'Albany, leaving her to dispose of them entirely according to her good pleasure. Among these papers was found a short letter, undated, addressed "To the friend I have left behind, Tommaso di Caluso, at Turin," and which ran as follows:—

"As I may any day give way beneath the very serious malady which is consuming me, I have thought it wise to prepare these few lines in order that they may be given to you as a proof that you have always, to my last moment, been present to my mind and very dear to my heart. The person whom above everything in the world I have most respected and loved, may some day tell you all the circumstances of my illness. I supplicate and conjure you to do your best to see and console her, and to concert with her the various measures which I have begged her to carry out with regard to my writings.

"I will not give you more pain, at present, by saying any more. I have known in you one of the most rare men in every respect. I die loving and esteeming you, and valuing myself for your friendship if I have deserved it. Farewell, farewell."

XVIII

FABRE

"H appiness has disappeared out of the world for me," wrote Mme. d'Albany, in January 1804, to her old friend Canon Luti, at Siena. "I take interest in nothing; the world might be completely upset without my noticing it. I read a little, and reading is the only thing which gives me any courage, a merely artificial courage; for when I return to my own thoughts and think of all that I have lost, I burst into tears and call Death to my assistance, but Death will not come. O God! what a misfortune to lose a person whom one adores and venerates at the same time. I think that if I still had Thérèse (Mme. Mocenni) it would be some consolation; but there is no consolation for me. I have the strength to hide my feelings before the world, for no one could conceive my misfortune who has not felt it. A twenty-six years' friendship with so perfect a being, and then to see him taken away from me at the very age when I required him most."

Alfieri a perfect being—a being adored and venerated by Mme. d'Albany! One cannot help, in reading these words, smiling sadly at the strange magic by which Death metamorphoses those whom he has taken in the eyes of the survivors; at the strange potions by means of which he makes love spring up in the hearts where it has ceased to exist, saving us from hypocrisy by making us really feel what is false to our nature, enabling us to lie to ourselves instead of lying to others. The Countess of Albany's grief was certainly most sincere; long after all direct references to Alfieri have ceased in her correspondence (I am speaking principally of that with her intimates at Siena), there reigns throughout her letters a depression, an indifference to everything, which shows that the world had indeed become empty in her eyes. But though the grief was sincere, I greatly question whether the love was so. Alfieri had become, in his later years, the incarnation of dreary violence; he could not have been much to anyone's feelings; and Mme. d'Albany's engrossment in her readings, in political news and town gossip, even with her most intimate correspondents, shows that Alfieri played but a very small part in her colourless life. So small a part, that one may say, without fear of injustice, that Mme. d'Albany had pretty well ceased to love him at all; for had she loved him, would she have been as indifferent, as serene as she appears in all her letters, while the man she loved was killing himself as certainly as if he were taking daily doses of a slow poison? Love is vigilant, love is full of fears, and Mme. d'Albany was so little vigilant, so little troubled by fears, that when this visibly dying man, this man who had prepared his epitaph, who had settled all his literary affairs, who had written the farewell letter to his friend, actually died, she would seem to have been thunder-stricken not merely by grief, but by amazement.

The Countess of Albany was not a selfish woman; she had, apparently without complaining, sacrificed her social tastes, made herself an old woman before her time, in acquiescence to Alfieri's misanthropic and routinist self-engrossment; she had been satisfied, or thought herself satisfied, with the cold, ceremonious adoration of a man who divided his time between his studies, his horses, and his intrigues with other women; but unselfish natures are often unselfish from their very thinness and coldness. Alfieri, heaven knows, had been selfish and self-engrossed; but, perhaps because he was selfish and self-engrossed, because he was always listening to his own ideas, and nursing his own feelings, Alfieri had been passionate and loving; and, as we have seen, while he seemed growing daily more fossilised, while he was at once engrossed with his own schemes of literary glory, and indifferently amusing himself by infidelities to his lady, he was then, even then, constantly haunted by the thought that, unless he himself were left behind in the terrors of widowhood, the Countess of Albany would have to suffer those pangs which he felt that he himself could never endure.

Alfieri saw the Countess through the medium of his own character, and he proved mistaken. Perhaps the most terrible ironical retribution which could have fallen upon his strange egomania, would have been, had such a thing been possible, the revelation of how gratuitous had been that terrible vision of Mme. d'Albany's life after his death; the revelation of how little difference, after the first great grief, his loss had made in her life; the revelation that, unnoticed, unconsciously, a successor had been prepared for him.

In a very melancholy letter, dated May 31, 1804, in which Mme. d'Albany expatiates to her friend Canon Luti upon the uselessness of her life, and her desire to end it, I find this unobtrusive little sentence: "Fabre desires his compliments to you. He has been a great resource to me in everything."

This sentence, I think, explains what to the enemies of Mme. d'Albany has been a delightful scandal, and to her admirers a melancholy mystery; explains, reduces to mere very simple, conceivable, neither commendable nor shameful every-day prose, the fact that little by little the place left vacant by Alfieri was filled by another man. Italian writers, inheriting from Giordani, even from Foscolo, a certain animosity against a woman who, as soon as Alfieri was dead, became once more what nature had made her, half French, with a great preference for French and French things—Italian writers, I say, have tried to turn the Fabre episode into something extremely disgraceful to Mme. d'Albany. Massimo d'Azeglio, partly out of hatred to the Countess, who was rather severe and acrimonious upon his youthful free-and-easiness, partly out of a desire to amuse his readers, has introduced into his autobiography an anecdote told him by Mme. de Prié (the niece of Alfieri's famous Turin mistress, and the lady who took it upon herself to send him a priest without consulting the Countess), to the effect that she had watched Fabre making eyes, kissing his fingers, and generally exchanging signals with Mme. d'Albany at a party where Alfieri was present. Let those who are amused by this piece of gossip believe it implicitly; it does not appear to me either amusing, or credible, or creditable to the man who retailed it. The Florentine society of the early years of this century was, if we may trust the keen observation of Stendhal, almost as naïvely and openly profligate as that of a South Sea Island village; and such a society, which could talk of the things and in the way which it did, which could permit certain poetical compositions (found highly characteristic by Stendhal) to be publicly performed before the ladies and gentlemen celebrated therein, such a society naturally enjoyed and believed a story like that retailed by d'Azeglio. But surely we may put it behind us, we who are not Florentines of the year 1800, and who can actually conceive that a woman who had exchanged irreproachable submission to a drunken husband, for legally unsanctioned, but open and faithful attachment for a man like Alfieri, might at the age of fifty take a liking to a man of thirty-five without that liking requiring a disgusting explanation. The clean explanation seems so much simpler and more consonant. Fabre had become an intimate of the house during Alfieri's last years. He was French, he was a painter; two high recommendations to Mme. d'Albany. He was, if we may trust Paul Louis Courier, who made him the hero of a famous imaginary dialogue, clever with a peculiarly French sort of cleverness; he gave the Countess lessons in painting while Alfieri was poring over his work. The sudden death of Alfieri would bring Fabre into still closer relations with Mme. d'Albany, as a friend of the deceased, the brother of his physician, and the virtual fellow-countryman of the Countess; he would naturally be called upon to help in a hundred and one melancholy arrangements: he received visitors, answered letters, gave orders; he probably laid Alfieri in his coffin. When all the bustle incident upon death had subsided, Fabre would remain Mme. d'Albany's most constant visitor. He, who had seen Alfieri at the very last, might be admitted when the door was closed to all others; he could help to sort the dead man's papers; he could, in his artistic capacity, discuss the plans for Alfieri's monument, write to Canova, correspond with the dignitaries of Santa Croce, and so forth; come in contact with the Countess in those manifold pieces of business, in those long conversations, which seem, for a time, to keep the dead one still in the company of the living. There is nothing difficult to understand or shameful to relate in all this; and the friends of the Countess, delicate-minded women like Mme. de Souza, puritanic-minded men like Sismondi, misanthropic or scoffing people like Foscolo or Paul Louis Courier, found nothing at which to take umbrage, nothing to rage or laugh at, in this long intimacy between a woman over fifty and a man many years her junior; a man who lived at the other end of Florence, who (if I may trust traditions yet alive) was supposed to be attached to a woman well known to Mme. d'Albany; nor have we, I think, any right to be less charitable than they.

Louise d'Albany, careless, like most women of her day, of social institutions, and particularly hostile to marriage, was certainly not an impure woman; her whole life goes to prove this. But Louise d'Albany was an indifferent woman, and the extinction of all youthful passion and enthusiasm, the friction of a cynical world, made her daily more indifferent. She had been faithful to Alfieri, devotedly enduring one of the most unendurable of companions, loving and admiring him while he was still alive. But once the pressure of that strong personality removed, the image of Alfieri appears to have been obliterated little by little from the soft wax of her character. She continued, nay instituted, a sort of cultus of Alfieri; became, as his beloved, the priestess presiding over what had once been his house, and was now his temple. The house on the Lung Arno remained the Casa Alfieri; the rooms which he had inhabited were kept carefully untouched; his books and papers were elaborated and preserved as he had left them; his portraits were everywhere, and visitors, like Foscolo, Courier, Sismondi, and the young Lamartine, were expected to inquire respectfully into the legend of the divinity, to ask to see his relics, as the visitors of a shrine might be expected to enquire into the legend, to ask to see the relics, of some great saint. Mme. d'Albany conscientiously devoted a portion of her time to seeing that Alfieri's works were properly published, and that Alfieri's tomb in Santa Croce was properly executed. She was, as I have said, the priestess, the divinely selected priestess, of the divinity. But at the same time Mme. d'Albany gradually settled down quite comfortably and happily without Alfieri. After the first great grief was over a sense of relief may have arisen, a sense that after all "'tis an ill wind that blows no good"; that if she had lost Alfieri she had gained a degree of liberty, of independence, that she had acquired a possibility of being herself with all her tastes, the very existence of which she had forgotten while living under the shadow of that strange and disagreeable great man. A negative sense of compensation, of pleasure in the foreign society to which she could now devote herself; of satisfaction in the miniature copy of her former Parisian salon which she could arrange in her Florentine house; of comfort in a gently bustling, unconcerned, cheerful old age; negative feelings which, perhaps as a result of their very repression, seem little by little to have turned to a positive feeling, a positive aversion for the past which she refused to regret, a positive dislike to the memory of the man whom she could no longer love. Horrible things to say; yet, I fear, true. A man such as Alfieri had permitted himself to become, admirable in many respects, but intolerant, hard, arrogant, selfish, self-engrossed, cannot really be loved; he may be endured as a result of long habit, he may inflict his personality without effort upon another; but in order that this be the case that other must be singularly apathetic, indifferent, malleable; and apathetic, indifferent, and malleable people, those who never resist the living individual, rarely remember the dead one. "She was," writes one of the most conscientious and respectful of men, the late Gino Capponi, "heavy in feature and form, and, if I may say so, her mind, like her body, was thick-set. . . Since several years she had ceased to love Alfieri."

We cannot be indignant with her; she had never pretended to be what she was not. A highly intellectual, literary mind, a pure temperament, a passive, rather characterless character, taking the impress of its surroundings; passionate when Alfieri was passionate, depressed when

Alfieri was depressed; cheerful when Alfieri's successors, Fabre and mankind and womankind in general, were cheerful. To be angry with such a woman would be ridiculous; but, little as we may feel attached to the memory of Alfieri, we cannot help saying to ourselves, "Thank Heaven he never understood what she was; thank Heaven he never foresaw what she would be!"

XIX

Salon of the Countess

A shadowy being, nay, a shadow cast in the unmistakable shape of another, so long as Alfieri was alive, the Countess of Albany seems to gain consistency and form, to become a substantive person, only after Alfieri's death. This woman, whom, in the last ten years, we have seen consorting almost exclusively with Italians, and spending the greater proportion of her days in solitary reading of Condillac, Lock, Kant, Mme. de Genlis, Lessing, Milton, everything and anything; whose letters, exclusively (as far as I know them) to Italians of the middle classes, are full of fury against everything that is French; this woman, who has hitherto been a feeble replica of Alfieri, suddenly turns into an extremely sociable, chatty woman of the world, and a woman of the world who is, to all intents and purposes, French.

To be the rallying point of a very cosmopolitan, literary, but by no means unworldly society, seems suddenly to have become Mme. d'Albany's mission; and reading the letters copied from the Montpellier Archives, and published by M. Saint René Taillandier, one wonders how this friend of Mme. de Staël, of Sismondi, of Mme. de Souza, this hostess of Moore, of Lamartine, of Lady Morgan, of every sort of French, English, German, Russian, or polyglot creature of distinction that travelled through Italy in the early part of this century, could ever have been the beloved of Alfieri, the misanthropic correspondent of a lot of Sienese professors, priests, and shop-keepers.

The fact was that Mme. d'Albany could now become, so to speak, what she really was; or, at least, show herself to be such. Worldly wise and a trifle cynical she had always been; in the midst of the pages of literary review and political newspaper constituting her letters to Mme. Mocenni, Canon Luti and Alessandro Cerretani of Siena, there is a good deal of mere personal gossip, stories of married women's lovers, married men's mistresses, domestic bickerings, &c., interspersed with very plain-spoken and (according to our ideas) slightly demoralised moralisings. It is evident that this was not a woman to shrink from the reality of things, to take the world in disgust, to expect too much of her acquaintances. On the other hand these letters of the Alfieri period show Mme. d'Albany to have been decidedly a good-natured and friendly woman. She has the gift of getting people to trust her with their little annoyances and grievances; she is constantly administering sympathy to Mme. Mocenni for the tiresomeness and stupidity and harshness of her husband; she keeps up a long correspondence, recommending books, correcting French exercises, exhorting to study and to virtue (particularly to abstinence from gambling), encouraging, helping Mme. Mocenni's boy Vittorio. She is clearly a woman who enjoys hearing about other folk's concerns, enjoys taking an interest in them, sympathising and, if possible, assisting them.

These two qualities, a dose of cynical worldliness, sufficient to prevent all squeamishness and that coldness and harshness which springs from expecting people to be better than they are, and a dose of kindliness, helpfulness, pleasure in knowing the affairs and feelings and troubles of others; these two qualities are, I should think, the essentials for a woman who would keep a salon in the old sense of the word, who would be the centre of a large but decidedly select society, the friend and correspondent of many and various people possessed of more genius or more character than herself. Such a woman, thanks to her easy-going knowledge of the world, and to her cordial curiosity and helpfulness, is the friend of the most hostile people; and she is so completely satisfied with, and interested in, the particular person with whom she is talking or to whom she is writing, that that particular person really believes himself or herself to be her chief friend, and overlooks the scores of other chief friends, viewed with exactly the same degree of interest, and treated with the same degree of cordiality all round. The world is apt to like such women, as such women like it, and to say of them that there must be an immense richness of character, an extraordinary power of bringing out the best qualities of every individual, in a woman who can drive such complicated teams of friends. But is it not more probable that the secret of such success is poverty of personality rather than richness; and that so many people receive a share of friendship, of sympathy, of comprehension, because each receives only very little; because the universal friend is too obtuse to mind anybody's faults, and too obtuse, also, to mind anybody's great virtues? In short, do not such women pay people merely in the paper money of attention, which can be multiplied at pleasure, rather than in the gold coin of sympathy, of which the supply is extremely small?

Be this as it may, Mme. d'Albany, after having been, in the earlier period of her life, essentially the woman who had one friend, who let the wax of her nature be stamped in one clear die, became, in the twenty years which separate the death of Alfieri from her own, pre-eminently the woman with many friends, a blurred personality in which we recognise traces of the mental effigy of many and various people. Mme. d'Albany was, therefore, in superficial sympathy with nearly everyone, and in deep antagonism with no one: she was the ideal of the woman who keeps a literary and political salon. At that time especially, when Italy was visited only by people of a certain social standing, society was carried on by a most complicated system of letters of introduction, and everyone of any note brought a letter to Mme. d'Albany. "*La grande lanterne magique passe tout par votre salon,*" wrote Sismondi to the Countess; and the metaphor could not be truer. Writers and artists, beautiful women, diplomatists, journalists, pedants, men of science, women of fashion, Châteaubriand and Mme. de Staël, Lamartine and Paul Louis Courier, Mme. Récamier and the Duchess of Devonshire, Canova and Foscolo, and Sismondi and Werner, the whole intellectual world of the Empire and the Restoration, all seem to be projected, figures now flitting past like shadows, now dwelling long, clear and coloured, upon the rather colourless and patternless background of Mme. d'Albany's house; nay, of Mme. d'Albany herself. Such readers as may wish to have all these figures, remembered or forgotten, pointed out to them, called by their right names and titles, treated with the perfect impartiality of a *valet de place* expounding monuments, or of a chamberlain announcing the guests at a *levée*, may refer to the two volumes of Baron Alfred von Reumont; and such readers (and I hope they are more numerous) as may wish to examine some of the nobler and more interesting of these projected shadows of men and women, may read with pleasure and profit the letters of Sismondi, Bonstetten, Mme. de Souza and Mme. de Staël to the Countess of Albany, and the interesting pages of criticism in which they have been imbedded by M. St.-René Taillandier. With regard to myself, I feel that the time and space which have been given me in order to analyse or reconstruct the curious type and curious individual called Louise d'Albany are both nearly exhausted; and I can therefore select to dwell upon, of these many magic-lantern men and women, of these friends of the Countess, only two, because they seem to me to exemplify my remarks about the friendship of a woman whose vocation it is to have many friends. The two are Sismondi and Foscolo.

Two or three years after Alfieri's death, somewhere about the year 1806 or 1807, there was introduced to Mme. d'Albany a sort of half-Italian, half-French Swiss, a man young in years and singularly young—with the peculiar earnestness, gravity, purity which belongs sometimes to youth—in spirit, Jean Charles Léonard Simonde de Sismondi. Quietly idealistic, with one of those northern, eminently Protestant minds which imagine the principle of good to be more solemnly serious, the principle of evil more vainly negative, than is, alas, the case in this world—M. de Sismondi, full of the heroism of mediæval Italy which he was studying with a view to his great work, came to the house of Alfieri, to the woman whom Alfieri had loved, as to things most reverend and almost sacred. The Countess of Albany received him very well; and this good reception, the motherly cordiality of this woman with that light in her hazel eyes, that welcoming graciousness in the lines of her mouth, which Lamartine has charmingly described, with the *"parole suave, manières sans apprêt, familiarité rassurante,"* "which made one doubt whether she was descending to the level of her visitor, or raising him up to her own,"—this reception by this woman, who was, moreover, still surrounded by a halo of Alfieri's glory, fairly conquered the heart, the pure, warm, grave and truthful heart of young Sismondi. He saw her often, on his way between Geneva, whither he was called by his family business and his lectures, and Pescia, a little town nestled among the olives of the Lucchese Apennine, where he was for ever sighing to join his mother, to resume his walks, his readings with this noble old woman. Florence, the house on the Lung Arno, had an almost romantic fascination for Sismondi; those passing visits, at intervals of months, when Mme. d'Albany would devote herself entirely to the traveller, sit chatting, or rather (we feel that) listening to the young man's enthusiastic talk about liberty, letters, and philanthropy, about Alfieri and Mme. de Staël, enabled Sismondi to make up for himself a sort of half-imaginary Countess of Albany, to whom he poured out all his hopes and fears in innumerable letters, for whom he longed as (alas!) we perhaps long only for the phantoms of our own creating. That Mme. d'Albany was, after all, a shallow woman; that she adored a mediocre M. Fabre (to whom Sismondi invariably sent respectful messages) and half disliked the memory of Alfieri; that she had called Mme. de Staël, Sismondi's goddess, about whom he was for ever expatiating, "a mad woman who always wants to inspire passions, and feels nothing, and makes her readers feel nothing" (I am quoting from an unpublished letter at Siena); that she preferred despotism on the whole to liberty, and had no particular belief or interest in the heroic things of the present and future; that she was a lover of gossip and scandal, sometimes (as Gino Capponi says) hard and disagreeable; that she inspired some men, like d'Azeglio and Giordani, with a positive repulsion as a vulgar-minded, spiteful, meddlesome old thing; that there should be any other Mme. d'Albany than the one of his noble fancy, than the woman whose image (fashioned by himself) he loved to unite with the image of his own sweet, serious, shy, noble-minded mother: all these things M. de Sismondi, who never guessed himself to be otherwise than the most unpoetical and practical of men, never dreamed of. So Sismondi went on writing to Mme. d'Albany, pouring out his grief at Mme. de Staël's persecutions, his schemes of general improvement, all the interests which filled his gentle, austere, and enthusiastic mind. 1814 came, and 1815. Sismondi had always hated, with the hatred of an Italian mediæval patriot, and the hatred of an eighteenth-century philanthropist, the despotism, the bureaucratic levelling, the great military slaughters of Napoleon; but when he saw Napoleon succeeded by the inept and wicked governments of the Restoration, his heart seemed to burst. A Swiss, scarcely acquainted with France, the passion for the principles of liberty and good sense and progress which France had represented, the passion for France itself, burst out in him with generous ardour. This man suffered intensely at what to him, as to Byron and to Shelley (we must recollect the introduction of the *Revolt of Islam*), seemed the battle between progress and retrogression; and suffered all the more as he was too pure and just-minded not to feel the impossibility of complete sympathy with either side. Mme. d'Albany answered his letters with Olympic serenity. What was it to her which got the upper hand? She was by this time one of those placid mixtures of optimism and pessimism which do not expect good to triumph, simply because they do not care whether good does triumph. Sismondi, in his adoration of her, thought this might be the result of a superior magnanimity of character; yet he kept conjuring her to take an interest in the tragedy which was taking place before her eyes. If she will take no interest, will not Fabre? "Does M. Fabre not feel himself turning French again?" writes Sismondi, and there is a pathetic insistency in the question. Fabre thought of his pictures, his collections of antiques, perhaps of his dinner; of anything save France and political events. Mme. d'Albany smiled serenely, and chaffed Sismondi a little for his political passions. Sismondi, of all men the most loyal to the idea he had formed of his friends, seems never to have permitted himself to see the real woman, the real abyss of indifference, beneath his ideal Mme. d'Albany. But there are few things more pathetic, I think, than the letters of this enthusiastic man to this cold woman; than the belief of Sismondi—writing that the retrograde measures of which he reads in the papers give him fits of fever, that the post days on which he expects political news are days of frenzied expectation—in the moral fibre, the faculty for indignation, of this pleasant, indifferent, cynical quasi-widow of Alfieri.

The story of the Countess and Foscolo is an even sadder instance of those melancholy little psychological dramas which go on, unseen to the world, in a man's soul; little dramas without outward events, without deaths or partings or such-like similar visible catastrophes, but the action of which is the slow murder of an affection, of an ideal, of a belief in the loyalty, sympathy, and comprehension of another. The character and history of Ugo Foscolo, like Chénier, half a Greek in blood, and more than half a Greek in passionate love of beauty and indomitable love of liberty, are amongst the most interesting in Italian literature; and I regret that I can say but little of them in this place. Reviewing his brief life, his long career from the moment when, scarcely more than a boy, he had entered the service of liberty as a soldier, a political writer, and a poet, only to taste the bitterness of the betrayal of Campo Formio, he wrote, in 1823, from London, where he was slowly dying, to his sister Rubina: "I am now nearly forty-six; and you, although younger than myself, can recollect how miserable, how unquiet and uncertain our lives have always been ever since our childhood." Poor, vain, passionate and proud, torn between the selfish impulses of an exactingly sensuous and imaginative nature, and the rigid sense of duty of a heroic and generous mind, Ugo Foscolo was one of the earliest and most genuine victims of that sickness of disappointed hope and betrayed enthusiasm, of that *Weltschmerz* of which personal misfortunes seemed as but the least dreadful part, that came upon the noblest minds after the Revolution, and which he has painted, with great energy and truthfulness, in his early novel *Jacopo Ortis*. His career broken by his determination never to come to terms with any sort of baseness, his happiness destroyed by political disappointment, literary feuds, and a number of love affairs into which his weaker, more passionate and vainer, yet not more ungenerous temper was for ever embroiling him, Foscolo came to Florence, ill and miserable, in the year 1812. The Countess of Albany, recognising in him a something—a mixture of independence, of passion, of vanity, of truthfulness, of pose—which resembled Alfieri in his earlier days (though, as she was unable to see, a nobler Alfieri, wider-minded, warmer-hearted, born in a nobler civilization and destined to give to Italy a nobler example, the pattern for her Leopardi, than Alfieri had been able to give)—the Countess of Albany received Foscolo well. His letters are full of allusions to the hours which he spent seated at the little round table in Mme. d'Albany's drawing-room, opposite to the "Muse" newly bought of Canova, narrating to her his many and tangled love affairs; love affairs in which he left his heart on all the briars, and in which, however, by an instinct which shows the very nobleness of his nature, he seems to have been impelled rather towards women whom he must love sincerely and unhappily, than towards Marchesa di Prié and Lady Ligonier, like Alfieri; love affairs in which, alas, there was also a good dose of the vanity of a poet and a notorious beau. Mme. d'Albany, as we have seen, loved gossip; and, being a kind, helpful woman, she also sincerely liked becoming the confidant of other folk's woes. She took a real affection for this strange Foscolo. Foscolo, in return, ill, sore of heart, solitary, gradually got to love this gentle, sympathising Countess with a sort of filial devotion, but a filial devotion into which there entered also somewhat of the feeling of a wounded man towards his nurse, of the feeling of a devout man towards his Madonna.

His letters are full of this feeling: "My friend and not the friend of my good fortune," he writes to Mme. d'Albany in 1813, "I seem to have left home, mother, friends, and almost the person dearest to my heart in leaving Florence." Again, "I had in you, *mia Signora*, a friend and a mother; a person, in short, such as no name can express, but such as sufficed to console me in the miseries which are perhaps incurable and interminable." Her letters are a real ray of sunlight in his gloomy life, they are "so full of graciousness, and condescension and benevolence and love. I venture to use this last word, because I feel the sentiment which it expresses in myself towards you."

His health, his work, his money-matters, his love-affairs, were all getting into a more and more lamentable condition, in which Mme. d'Albany's sympathy came as a blessing, when the catastrophes of

1814 and 1815, which to Italy meant the commencement of a state of degradation and misery much more intolerable and hopeless than any previous one, came and drowned the various bitternesses of poor Foscolo's life in a sea of bitterness. "Italy," wrote Foscolo to Mme. d'Albany in 1814, "is a corpse; and a corpse which must not be touched if the stench thereof is not to be made more horrible. And yet I see certain crazy creatures fantasticating ways of bringing her to life; for myself, I should wish her to be buried with myself, and overwhelmed by the seas, or that some new Phaeton should precipitate upon her the flaming heavens, so that the ashes should be scattered to the four winds, and that the nations coming and to come should forget the infamy of our times. Amen."

How strongly we feel in this outburst that, despite his despair, or perhaps on account of it, Foscolo is himself one of those "crazy creatures fantasticating ways of bringing Italy to life!" But the Countess did not understand; she could conceive liking Bonaparte and serving him, or liking the Restoration and serving it; but to love an abstract Italy which did not yet exist, to hate equally all those who deprived it of freedom, that was not within her comprehension. And as she could not comprehend this feeling, the mainspring of Foscolo's soul, so she could understand of Foscolo only the slighter, meaner things: his troubles and intrigues, his loves and quarrels. The moment came when the grief of miscomprehension was revealed to poor Foscolo; when he saw how little he was understood by this woman whom he loved as a mother. Foscolo had refused, latterly, to serve Napoleon; he refused, also, to serve the Austrians. Hated for his independent ways both by the Bonapartists and the reactionists, surrounded by spies, he was forced to quit Italy never to return. He wrote to explain his motives to Mme. d'Albany. Mme. d'Albany wrote back in a way which showed that she believed the assertions of Foscolo's enemies; that she ascribed to cowardice, to meanness, to a base desire to make himself conspicuous, the self-inflicted exile which he had taken upon him: a letter which the editor of Foscolo's correspondence describes to us in one word—unworthy.

This letter came upon Foscolo like a thunder-clap. "So thus," he wrote to the Countess in August 1815, "generosity and justice are banished even from nobler souls. Your letter, Signora Contessa, grieves me, and confers upon me, at the same time, two advantages: it diminishes suddenly the perpetual nostalgia which I have felt for Florence, and it affords me an occasion to try my strength of spirit. . . My hatred for the tyranny with which Bonaparte was oppressing Italy does not imply that I should love the house of Austria. The difference for me was that I hoped that Bonaparte's ambition might bring about, if not the independence of Italy, at least such magnanimous deeds as might raise the Italians; whereas the regular government of Austria precludes all such hopes. I should be mad and infamous if I desired for Italy, which requires peace at any price, new disorders and slaughterings; but I should consider myself madder still and more infamous if, having despised to serve the foreigner who has fallen, I should accept to serve the foreigner who has succeeded. . . But if your accusation of inconstancy is unjust, your accusation that I want to '*passer pour original*' is actually offensive and mocking."

Later, in his solitary wanderings, Foscolo's heart seems to have melted towards his former friend; he wrote her one or two letters, conciliating, friendly, but how different from the former ones! The Countess of Albany, whom he had loved and trusted, was dead; the woman who remained was dear to him as a mere relic of that dead ideal.

Such is the story of Mme. d'Albany's friendship for two of the noblest spirits, Sismondi and Foscolo, of their day; the noblest, the one in his pure austerity, the other in his magnanimous passionateness, that ever crossed the path of the beloved of Alfieri.

SANTA CROCE

With her other friends, who gave less of their own heart and asked less of hers, Mme. d'Albany was more fortunate. She contrived to connect herself by correspondence with the most eminent men and women of the most different views and tempers; she made her salon in Florence, as M. St. René Taillandier has observed, a sort of adjunct to the cosmopolitan salon of Mme. de Staël at Coppet. Her efforts in so doing were crowned with the very highest success. In 1809 Napoleon requested Mme. d'Albany to leave Florence for Paris, where, he added with a mixture of brutality and sarcasm, she might indulge her love of art in the new galleries of the Louvre, and where her social talents could no longer spread dissatisfaction with his government, as was the case in Italy.

The one year's residence in Paris, which Napoleon's jealous meddlesomeness forced upon her, was, in itself, a very enjoyable time, spent with the friends whom she had left in '93, and with a whole host of new ones whom she had made since. She returned to Florence with a larger number of devoted correspondents than ever; her salon became more and more brilliant; and when, after Waterloo, the whole English world of politics, fashion, and letters poured on to the Continent, her house became, as Sismondi said, the wall on which all the most brilliant figures of the great magic lantern were projected.

Thus, seeing crowds of the most distinguished and delightful people, receiving piles of the most interesting and adoring letters, happy, self-satisfied, Mme. d'Albany grew into an old woman. Every evening until ten, the rooms of the Casa Alfieri were thrown open; the servants in the Stuart liveries ushered in the guests, the tea was served in those famous services emblazoned with the royal arms of England. The Countess had not yet abandoned her regal pretensions; for all her condescending cordiality towards the elect, she could assume airs of social superiority which some folk scarcely brooked, and she was evidently pleased when, half in earnest, Mme. de Staël addressed her as "My dear Sovereign," "My dear Queen," and even when that vulgar woman of genius, Lady Morgan, made a buffoonish scene about the "dead usurper," on the death of George III. But Mme. d'Albany herself was getting to look and talk less and less like a queen, either the Queen of Great Britain or the Queen of Hearts; she was fat, squat, snub, dressed with an eternal red shawl (now the property of an intimate friend of mine), in a dress extremely suggestive of an old house-keeper. She was, when not doing the queen, cordial, cheerful in manner, loving to have children about her, to spoil them with cakes and see them romp and dance; free and easy, cynical, Rabelaisian, if I may use the expression, as such mongrel Frenchwomen are apt to grow with years; the nick-name which she gave to a member of a family where the tradition of her and her ways still persists, reveals a wealth of coarse fun which is rather strange in a woman who was once the Beatrice or Laura of a poet. She was active, mentally and bodily, never giving up her multifarious reading, her letter-writing; never foregoing her invariable morning walk, in a big bonnet and the legendary red shawl, down the Lung Arno and into the Cascine.

Such was Louise of Stolberg, Countess of Albany, widow of Prince Charles Edward, widow, in a sense, of the poet Vittorio Alfieri; and such, at the age of seventy-two, did death overtake her, on the 29th January 1824. Her property she bequeathed to Fabre whom a false rumour had called her husband; and Fabre left it jointly to his native town of Montpellier, and to his friend the Cavaliere Emilio Santarelli, who still lives and recollects Mme. d'Albany.

The famous epitaph, composed by Alfieri for himself, had been mangled by Mme. d'Albany and those who helped her and Canova in devising his tomb; the companion epitaph, the one in which Alfieri described the Countess as buried next to him, was also mangled in its adaptation to a tomb erected in Santa Croce, entirely separate from Alfieri's. On that monument of Mme. d'Albany, in the chapel where moulder the frescoes of Masolino, there is not a word of that sentence of Alfieri's about the dead woman having been to him dearer and more respected than any other human thing. Mme. d'Albany had changed into quite another being between 1803 and 1824; the friend of Sismondi, of Foscolo, of Mme. de Staël, the worldly friend of many friends, seemed to have no connection with the lady who had wept for Alfieri in the convent at Rome, who had borne with all Alfieri's misanthropic furies after the Revolution, any more than with the delicate intellectual girl whom Charles Edward had nearly done to death in his drunken jealousy. So, on the whole, Fabre, and whosoever assisted Fabre, was right in concocting a new epitaph.

But to us, who have followed the career—whose lesson is that of the meanness which lurks in noble things, the nobility which lurks in mean ones—of this woman from her inauspicious wedding-day to the placid day of her death, to us Louise of Stolberg, Countess of Albany, Queen of Great Britain, France, and Ireland, will remain, for all blame we may give her and her times, a figure to remember and reflect upon, principally because of those suppressed words of her epitaph: *"A Victorio Alferio ultra res omnes dilecta, et quasi mortale numen ab ipso constanter habita et observata."*

A Note About the Author

Vernon Lee (1856–1935) was the pen name of Violet Paget, a British author of supernatural fiction. Born in France to British expatriate parents, Paget spent most of her life in continental Europe. A committed feminist and pacifist, she joined the Union of Democratic Control during the First World War to express her opposition to British militarism. A lesbian, Paget had relationships with Mary Robinson, Amy Levy, and Clementina Anstruther-Thomson throughout her life. Paget, a dedicated follower of Walter Pater's Aesthetic movement, lived for many years in Florence, where she gained a reputation as a leading scholar of the Italian Renaissance. In addition to her work in art history, Paget was a leading writer of short fiction featuring supernatural figures and themes. Among her best known works are *Hauntings* (1890), a collection of four chilling tales, and "Prince Alberic and the Snake Lady," a story which appeared in an 1895 issue of *The Yellow Book*, a controversial periodical that featured the works of Aubrey Beardsley, George Gissing, Henry James, and William Butler Yeats. Although Paget was largely forgotten by the mid-twentieth century, feminist scholars have rekindled attention in her pioneering work as a leading proponent of Aestheticism.

A Note from the Publisher

Spanning many genres, from non-fiction essays to literature classics to children's books and lyric poetry, Mint Edition books showcase the master works of our time in a modern new package. The text is freshly typeset, is clean and easy to read, and features a new note about the author in each volume. Many books also include exclusive new introductory material. Every book boasts a striking new cover, which makes it as appropriate for collecting as it is for gift giving. Mint Edition books are only printed when a reader orders them, so natural resources are not wasted. We're proud that our books are never manufactured in excess and exist only in the exact quantity they need to be read and enjoyed.

Discover more of your favorite classics with Bookfinity™.

- Track your reading with custom book lists.
- Get great book recommendations for your personalized Reader Type.
- Add reviews for your favorite books.
- AND MUCH MORE!

Visit **bookfinity.com** and take the fun Reader Type quiz to get started.

Enjoy our classic and modern companion pairings!